The ASQC Basic References in Quality Control: Statistical Techniques
John A. Cornell, PhD, and Samuel S. Shapiro, PhD, Editors

Volume 12: How to Choose the Proper Sample Size

by

Gary G. Brush

American Society for Quality Control
310 West Wisconsin Avenue
Milwaukee, Wisconsin 53203

Volume 12: How to Choose the Proper Sample Size

by

Gary G. Brush

ISBN 0-87389-050-7

Printed in the United States of America

The ASQC Basic References in Quality Control: Statistical Techniques is a continuing literature project of ASQC's Statistics Division. Its aim is to present the latest statistical techniques in a form which is easily followed by the quality control practitioner so that these procedures can be readily applied to solve industrial quality problems.

Suggestions as to subject matters to be covered and format of the booklets are welcome and will be considered in future editions. Such suggestions should be sent to one of the co-editors.

Volumes Published

How to Analyze Data with Simple Plots (W. Nelson)
How to Perform Continuous Sampling (CSP) (K. Stephens)
How to Test Normality and Other Distributional Assumptions (S. Shapiro)
How to Perform Skip-Lot and Chain Sampling (K. Stephens)
How to Run Mixture Experiments for Product Quality (J. Cornell)
How to Analyze Reliability Data (W. Nelson)
How and When to Perform Bayesian Acceptance Sampling (T. W. Calvin)
How to Apply Response Surface Methodology (J. Cornell)
How to Use Regression Analysis in Quality Control (D. C. Crocker)
How to Plan an Accelerated Life Test — Some Practical Guidelines (W. Meeker and G. Hahn)
How to Perform Statistical Tolerance Analysis (N. Cox)

In order to purchase volumes write to: American Society for Quality Control, 310 West Wisconsin Avenue, Milwaukee, Wisconsin 53203, USA.

FOREWORD

The ASQC Series, *Basic References in Quality Control: Statistical Techniques*, is a literature project of the Statistics Division of ASQC. The series' Review Board consists of Saul Blumenthal, Joseph W. Foster, Alan J. Gross, Gerald J. Hahn, Norman L. Johnson, Alan Lasater, Edward A. Sylvestre, and Harrison M. Wadsworth, Jr., supplemented (for the current volume, twelfth in the series) by Samuel Shapiro.

In the Statistics Division newsletter, volume 1, number 1 (February 21, 1980), Philip B. Crosby (then president of ASQC) called the comprehension and handling of statistics ". . . the most basic of needs for all of us . . . ." He went on to state that "Without numerical information in its most precise form, we cannot complete our responsibility to management and other fellow employees. And without the tools to first comprehend and then explain the analysis, we are equally impotent."

This booklet describes in a clear, *how-to* format the procedures necessary to select the appropriate sample size for a variety of problems that frequently occur in quality assurance and reliability problems. The booklet is organized into the general kinds of problems addressed: estimating one parameter, comparing two parameters, selecting the better of two parameters, testing a hypothesis about one parameter, constructing tolerance intervals, and making economically based decisions. Graphs are given that facilitate the selection of sample size and comparison of alternatives.

The author has had 18 years of experience in many phases of quality assurance activities, including: quality engineering of transmission and switching equipment; conducting field reliability studies and reliability modeling; and development of statistical methods, software, and information systems for quality assurance applications. Mr. Brush currently works in telecommunications reliability and quality assurance; his current assignment is the managing of a group responsible for developing reliability requirements for switching equipment and conducting reliability analyses of telecommunications equipment and networks. He is a member of the ASQC, and has authored numerous published papers in the quality and reliability disciplines. He received the B.S. degree in statistics and computer science from the University of Delaware and the M.S. degree in mathematical statistics from Rutgers University.

John A. Cornell
University of Florida
Gainesville, Florida

PREFACE

The quality engineer is frequently faced with the problem of determining the appropriate sample size for a process characterization study, field reliability study, laboratory test, etc. Today there are available numerous texts and articles that provide equations that might be used to solve individual problems; yet one may find it helpful to develop graphical aids for some of the commonly occurring problems. These graphical aids facilitate comparing alternatives, making tradeoffs, and arriving at conclusions.

This text is a compilation of these graphical aids. The contribution here is the transformation of existing but often-cumbersome theory into easy-to-use curves. This booklet offers no contribution to the theoretical aspects of this subject; rather, its contents rest on the shoulders of those who have.

CONTENTS

1. INTRODUCTION

1.1 Statistical inference

Informed decision making relies on the collection of data and the making of statistical inferences from the data. Computer manufacturers inspect incoming samples of integrated circuits before assembling them on printed wiring boards to ascertain conformance with quality requirements. Drug manufacturers test new products on carefully selected target groups of animals or people before making those products available to the general population. Telecommunications researchers conduct laboratory tests to compare the reliability of several new laser transmitter configurations. Market researchers perform studies to understand customer needs and preferences.

In each of these cases data are collected and used to make a decision through statistical inference. From independent observations on (typically) a small number of units, a conclusion is drawn about the (typically) much larger population of which they are a part. The assumption that the observations are independent is critical; the assumption of independence should always be verified. There are two kinds of errors that can be made in these situations: errors due to bias and errors due to sampling.

Errors due to bias arise because the experiment or test does not exactly match the situation about which the conclusions are to be drawn. The reliability experiment of the laser transmitters might take place in the laboratory, whereas the intended application of the transmitters might be in a less-controlled environment. A drug might have different effects on people than on the mice in an experiment. The sampling of integrated circuits might have involved only samples from one of several suppliers being used. And the market researchers might have interviewed people who were not likely to buy the product being studied. These are just a few examples of causes of bias. An experiment or test can be devised to minimize errors due to bias by controlling test conditions so they will be as close as possible to the situation about which inferences are to be made.

Errors due to sampling arise because the sampled items rarely reflect exactly the characteristics of the entire population. Errors due to sampling can be controlled by specifying, in advance, the number of units to be included in the experiment or test. This is the topic of this text.

1.2 Categories of inference

It has been my experience that a large proportion of the statistical inferences required in the quality engineering field fall into five categories

1. Estimating one parameter

2. Comparing two parameters

3. Selecting the better of two parameters

4. Testing a hypothesis about one parameter

5. Constructing tolerance limits

In some of these categories, economical considerations can be useful.

There is a subtle difference between comparing and selecting. In selecting, we must pick one of the options. In comparing, we are permitted to conclude that there is no significant difference between the two options.

The primary focus is the discussion of graphical aids to help specify sample sizes that will control errors due to sampling at required levels for these five situations.

1.3 Parameters of interest

It has further been my experience that a large proportion of the statistical inferences required in the quality engineering field deal with three parametric situations:

1. Proportions (e.g., percent defective, percent dead on arrival). In this case, the distribution frequently assumed to be appropriate is the binomial distribution. The observed data take the form of a number of units, each of which either does or does not possess a characteristic of interest.

2. Rate (e.g., failures per hour, defects per 100 units). In this case, the Poisson distribution is frequently assumed to be appropriate. The observed data take the form of counts and a measure of "exposure" to the rate.

3. Mean and/or variance of a continuous distribution. Frequently the normal distribution is assumed to be appropriate. The observed data take the form of a number of units and a "reading" or "measurement" associated with each.

1.4 Use of curves

The curves presented here should be used as general guidelines on appropriate sample sizes, e.g., the curves would be useful for determining whether 100 or 500 units should be included in an experiment but *not* for choosing whether to have a sample size of 65 or a sample size of 70. The reasons for this are:

1. Many of the sample sizes are determined from equations that are approximations made to theoretical results so that calculations would be possible.

2. Many of the theoretical results are based on distributional assumptions and are sensitive to these assumptions, but in practice we will rarely be able to ascertain the validity of the assumptions.

2. ESTIMATING ONE PARAMETER

2.1 Overview of estimation

Estimation problems are characterized by tests or experiments in which the purpose is to construct a confidence interval for a parameter of interest. A confidence interval may be thought of as a range of parameter values that are consistent with the observed data. The interval is defined by a lower limit L and an upper limit U. Associated with the interval is a percentage (Q), which is called the confidence level. The strict definition of the confidence interval is that if the process of gathering data and calculating confidence intervals were repeated a great many times, then the true value of the parameter would be contained in the interval in $Q\%$ of the cases. This does *not* mean that for any *one* particular experiment or test the probability statement holds. This is a subtle but important point to remember.

There are two types of results that can occur from sampling error. First, our interval might not include the true, unknown parameter. Second, the interval might be too wide and, therefore, might include too many parameter values different from the true, unknown one. The first error will be controlled by specifying the desired confidence level. The second error is a function of the sample size and, therefore, can be controlled by specifying the required sample size.

2.2 Estimating one proportion

This case deals with estimating one proportion, e.g., percentage of units that are initially defective, percentage of units that fail outside the warranty period. We will assume that the proportion is expressed as a percent on the scale 0 to 100; the obvious translation can be made to the scale 0 to 1. When the experiment or test is completed, an estimate will be obtained of the true, unknown parameter p; call the estimate $\hat{p}$. A confidence interval will be constructed: $(\hat{p} - a, \hat{p} + b)$. If it is a 90% confidence interval, for example, and if we were to repeat the procedure a large number of times, then the constructed confidence intervals would contain the true, unknown value 90% of the time.

Certainly the narrower the confidence interval is, the more information is conveyed and the more useful it is in making decisions. So one way to establish some sense of precision in the interval is to require the interval in advance to be a prescribed length. Now if we let $\Delta = \dfrac{a + b}{2}$, then the length of the confidence interval is 2Δ. Notice that if $a = b$, then the confidence interval is symmetric: $(\hat{p} - \Delta, \hat{p} + \Delta)$.

Figures 1 through 4A show minimum sample sizes for various values of Δ and confidence levels of 80%, 90%, 95%, and 99%. The abscissa on the curves is a prior estimated bound on p. For example, if we knew through prior experience with a similar situation that p would be at most 10%, then we would reference the curves using an abscissa of 10. The sample size curves are symmetric about 50%, so we need to draw only one half of the scale from 0% to 100%. For example, if we knew that p would be 90% or more, we would reference the curves through the abscissa of 10.

The sample size curves reach a maximum at 50% and decrease as we move away from 50%. Therefore, the farther away from 50% we can bound p, the smaller the sample size required. If we have no basis on which to know a priori into what range p is likely to fall, then we should reference the curves through an abscissa of 50%.

In this and some of the other cases dealing with proportions, we actually have a set of dual figures: 1, 1A, 2, 2A, etc. This is in recognition of the fact that quality control applications frequently need to deal with smaller values of proportions than do, say, sample surveys for market research purposes. To make the curves most useful, one set is included for values of proportion of less than

3

10% and another set gives a fuller range (up to 50%). The figure numbers with the A appended give the smaller values of proportions.

2.2.1 Example

We need to estimate the percentage of a shipment of a certain piece part that is initially defective at the time the piece parts are received from the supplier. Our recent experience with the supplier and the specific piece part leads us to believe that the percentage will be, at most, 10%. For our estimate to be of use to us, we require that Δ, the half-width of the 90% confidence interval, be at most 2%. In Figure 2, for $\Delta=2$ and an abscissa of 10, we see that 600 is the required sample size.

2.2.2 Important points

1. If one is to err in the estimated bounds, one should err toward 50% rather than away from it.

2. Because of the bounding of p, the confidence levels are *at least* those given; for example, at least 90%, at least 95%.

3. The approximation used here loses accuracy rapidly as p gets very close to 0.

2.2.3 Curve equation

Figures 1 through 4A are based on the following equation, which is given in Mace (1974):

$$n = \left[\frac{Z\left[\frac{1+A}{2}\right]}{arcsin\left[\frac{\Delta/100}{\sqrt{\frac{p_B(100-p_B)}{10000}}}\right]} \right]^2 \tag{2.1}$$

where $Z(\chi)$ satisfies:

$$\int_{-\infty}^{Z(\chi)} \frac{1}{\sqrt{2\pi}} e^{-\frac{t^2}{2}} \, dt = \chi. \tag{2.2}$$

So $Z(\chi)$ is an upper quantile of a standard normal distribution. A is the confidence level expressed as a proportion and p_B is the estimated bound for p. For example, for the 95% confidence level, A is 0.95.

2.3 Estimating one rate

This case deals with estimating the rate at which a certain event occurs. The rate might be, e.g., the failure rate of an electronic component, mortality rate of a certain species of animals, or rate at which telephone calls are made. In cases involving rates, we will need to use two sets of curves. The first set will tell us how many events we need to see in our experiment; the second set will help us determine how many units we need to put on test so that we will be very certain of observing the required number of events in a specified period of time. This second set is useful, for example, in a laboratory experiment--we don't want to start a laboratory experiment knowing only that we have to continue it until 15 of the electronic components have failed. We need to know how many components we should include in the experiment so that, for example, it is very likely that 15 will fail within two weeks.

4

In the case of rates, we will be interested in obtaining a *relative* precision in the estimate of our rate, with a specified level of confidence. In the case of proportions, the precision was an *absolute* precision, e.g., the confidence interval might be 15% ± 2% or (13%, 17%). In the case of rates, the confidence interval will take the form of 7 per hour ± 5% (of the 7) or (6.65, 7.35). Figure 5 shows the number of events that need to be observed for various values of precision and confidence levels. The precision of .25, for example, means that the confidence interval would be (0.75X, 1.25X).

Figures 6 through 8 show how many units must be included in a study or test so that the probability is high that the required number of events will be observed in a prescribed time. These curves were initially developed for use with the Product Performance Surveys of telephone sets (Hiering and Hooke [1978]), where the typical length of the study might be 6 to 12 months. To make use of these curves, we need to have some idea of what the true failure rate is. If some other length of study is needed or some other values or units of failure rates are appropriate, then instead of using the curves in Figures 6 through 8, equation (2.4), given in Section 2.3.3 should be used.

2.3.1 Example

Suppose that a manufacturer of personal computer hard disks is interested in estimating their failure rate. The manufacturer wants to obtain a precision of 30% at the 95% confidence level. In Figure 5, at an abscissa of 0.3 (30%) on the 95% confidence level curve, we see that about 40 failures must be observed. Further suppose that we wish to have the study conclude within 12 months and that a reliability prediction gives us an estimate of 8% per year. Then in Figure 8, if we use an abscissa of 8 and look between the F=30 and F=50 curves, we see that if 700 units are included in the study, we will be pretty sure that within the 12 months the required number of failures will be observed.

2.3.2 Important points

1. In most of the discussion involving event rates, we will be using failure rates, because that is the most frequent application in reliability and quality assurance problems. We will talk about observing a certain number of "failures." However, all of the methods are applicable to event rates and events in general.

2. The assumption is made that the failure rate is constant over time. Even for very large sample sizes, the procedure for determining sample sizes is sensitive (nonrobust) to departures from this assumption. As a result, if we know that the failure rate is high for one time period (e.g., early life) and low for a different time period (e.g., steady-state), then we should do separate analyses on each period.

3. The theory also assumes that the study will be truncated when the Fth failure is observed. In practice, the study may instead run for a specified period of time. The theory used then may be only an approximation to the practice.

4. If the Fth failure is not observed in the specified time period, it would be wise to increase the length of the study until it is observed.

5. Once the required number of failures, F, has been determined, the sample size is then often selected by dividing F by the product of the failure rate and the desired length of the study. The difficulty with this approach, which corresponds *approximately* to $\gamma=.5$ in equation (2.4) below, is that the chance of observing the required number of failures in the desired amount of time is only 50%. Figures 6 through 8 are based on having a very good chance (95%) of doing so. It has been my experience that this latter approach is more appropriate in planning laboratory experiments, field reliability studies, and so on.

2.3.3 Curve equations

The curves in Figure 5 are based on the following equation, which is derived by Swann (1975):

$$F = 4 \left[\frac{Z\left(\frac{1+A}{2}\right)}{\ln\left(\frac{1+p}{1-p}\right)} \right]^2 \qquad (2.3)$$

where A is the confidence level expressed as a proportion and p is the desired precision. The curves in Figures 6 through 8 are based upon the following equation, derived by Swann (1975):

$$n = \frac{F + Z(\gamma)\sqrt{F}}{8.3 \cdot 10^{-4} \lambda T} + \frac{F}{2} \qquad (2.4)$$

where

F	is the number of failures;
λ	is the prior estimate of the failure rate in failures per hundred units per year;
T	is the number of months the study will last;
n	is the required sample size;
$Z(\chi)$	is an upper quantile of a standard normal distribution; and
γ	is the probability that the required number of failures is observed in the specified time.

In Figures 6 through 8, γ was chosen to be .95, so that there is a 95% chance that the required number of failures would be seen in the specified time interval. If the failure rates are expressed in units other than those used above, or a different value of γ is desired, then the equation for n must be adjusted accordingly.

2.4 Estimating the mean of one normal distribution

This case deals with estimating the mean of a normal distribution where the variance of the distribution may not be known. This problem may be appropriate in estimating the average thickness of gold plating on a population of contact fingers on printed circuit boards, the average weight of a species of animal, the average number of characters a print head can print before wearing out, and so on.

We will be interested in specifying a value of precision to control the length of the confidence interval. The confidence interval will be absolute, in the sense that the interval will take the form $X \pm \delta$. (Compare this with the *relative* definition in the rates case described earlier.)

Figure 9 is applicable in this case and is accessed by the precision ratio $\dfrac{\delta}{\sigma'}$, where σ' is a prior estimate of the true (possibly) unknown standard deviation of the distribution.

2.4.1 Example

Suppose we wish to estimate the average thickness of gold plating on a population of contact fingers on printed circuit boards. We specify that we want the half-width of the 90% confidence interval to be at most 5 microns, and we have information from other similar populations that tells us that 25 microns is a good estimate of the standard deviation. So $\delta=5$, $\sigma'=25$; then, in Figure 9, for a precision of $5/25 = 0.2$ and the 90% confidence level, we see that a sample size of approximately 70 contact fingers is required.

2.4.2 Important points

Whether or not the variable of interest is normally distributed, the mean of n independent identically distributed random variables will approach a normal distribution as n becomes large. So the determination of appropriate sample sizes is insensitive to departures from normality, at least for large sample sizes,

2.4.3 Curve equations

The curves in Figure 9 are based on the following procedure, outlined in Mace (1974). A first approximation is obtained by

$$n' = \left[\frac{Z\left(\frac{1+A}{2}\right)}{\frac{\delta}{\sigma'}} \right]^2 . \tag{2.5}$$

Then, starting with $n=n'$, n is increased until a value of n is found for which the following equation holds to the required degree of approximation:

$$n = \left[\frac{t\left(n-1;\frac{1+A}{2}\right)}{\frac{\delta}{\sigma'}} \right]^2 \tag{2.6}$$

where $t(m;y)$ is the $100\%y$ quantile of the central t-distribution with m degrees of freedom, and A is the confidence level expressed as a proportion. This value of n found is then the appropriate sample size. Hopefully, the range of values in Figure 9 is sufficient that the reader will not have to worry about this iteration; the explanation of how the curves were derived is included for completeness. One simple way of performing the iteration described above is illustrated in the following flowchart:

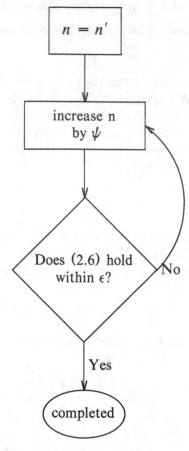

2.5 Estimating the variance of one normal distribution

In this case we are interested in estimating the variance of a normal distribution. This might be useful, for example, in setting acceptance limits for the inspection of materials being used in a manufacturing process or for estimating the precision of a measuring device. We wish to control the confidence interval to have a certain width or less. The confidence interval will be of the form $X \pm Y\%$ (of X). So we again have the concept of *relative*, rather than *absolute*, precision here. Figure 10 is appropriate for this case, and is accessed by the relative precision and confidence level required.

2.5.1 Example

Suppose we wish to estimate the variance of the population of inside diameters of washers. We want the 99% confidence interval to have a relative width of 0.2 or less. In Figure 10, for an abscissa of 0.2 and on the 99% curve, we see that a sample size of a little more than 300 is needed.

2.5.2 Important points

1. Even for large sample sizes, the determination of sample sizes is sensitive to departures from the normality assumption. For distributions that have lighter tails than the normal distribution, the computed sample sizes will be too large. Conversely, for distributions that have heavier tails than the normal distribution, the computed sample sizes will be too small.

2. The estimation of variance is sensitive to "outlier" data, that is, data that are vastly different from others in the sample. One simple way of determining the effect of such an outlier is to temporarily remove the data from the sample and notice the change in the resulting estimate.

More formal means of detecting and dealing with outliers are given in texts on data analysis, for example, Tukey (1977).

2.5.3 Curve equations

The curves in Figure 10 are based on the following equation, given in Mace (1974):

$$n = 1.5 + Z \left[\frac{1+A}{2} \right]^2 \left[\frac{1}{R} \left[\frac{1}{R} + \sqrt{\frac{1}{R^2} - 1} \right] - 0.5 \right] \qquad (2.7)$$

where R is the precision ratio and A is the confidence level expressed as a proportion.

3. COMPARING TWO PARAMETERS

3.1 Overview of comparison

The comparison problems considered here are a special kind of hypothesis testing. We will select the sample sizes to control several errors that can be made in hypothesis testing.

		TRUTH	
		Parameters are equal	Parameters are different
ACTION	Conclude that parameters are equal	No error	Type II error
	Conclude that parameters are different	Type I error	No error

As the above table illustrates, in comparing situations, we can err when we conclude either that the two parameters are different when they are, in fact, equal, or that the two parameters are equal when they are, in fact, different. Typically these two errors are called Type I and Type II errors, respectively. Experiments or studies are typically constructed to keep these errors at low levels, for example, 5% or 10%. The experiment would be described as having, for example, a probability of a Type I error of 5% and a probability of a Type II error of 10% for a certain set of "different" parameters. In this text we will use slightly different notation to maintain similarity with the confidence levels of the previous chapter. When a test has a probability of a Type I error of $X\%$, we will say that it is a test at the $(100-X)\%$ Type I level, and similarly for Type II errors. Thus we will speak of the 95% Type I level, and so on.

As mentioned earlier, we must specify an "alternative" to equality in the definition of the Type II level. For example, we might say, when the larger parameter is twice the smaller, we want to have a 95% chance of concluding from the data that the larger parameter is indeed larger than the smaller. This alternative will be stated slightly differently in the various cases discussed below to be compatible with the theory.

Hypothesis tests are usually formally specified by stating a null hypothesis (H_0) and an alternative (H_A). When the data fall into a region consistent with H_0, we will not reject the null hypothesis. When the data fall into a region inconsistent with H_0, we will reject it in favor of H_A.

We also need to make the distinction here between one-sided and two-sided tests. In this context, a one-sided test is used when we know the ordering of the two parameters; for example we know that X is larger than *or equal to Y*, and we want to design the test so that we will reject the hypothesis of equality with high probability when X is, for example, twice Y. In this context, a two-sided test is used when we don't know the ordering of the two parameters. In this case we might want to reject the hypothesis of equality with high probability either when X is twice Y or when Y is twice X. Because we have less prior information about the two parameters in the two-sided case compared to the one-sided case and we have two rejection requirements rather than one, the sample sizes required will be higher for the two-sided case for equal probabilities of a Type I error.

Curves have been provided for both the two-sided (Figures 14 through 16, 20 through 22, and 26 through 28) and the one-sided (Figures 11 through 13, 17 through 19, and 23 through 25) cases for proportions, rates, and means, but for only the one-sided case (Figures 29 through 31) for variances. This is in accordance with my experience in quality and reliability applications. For the reader interested in the two-sided comparison of variances, Chapter 5 of Mace (1974) covers the topic. Also, we shall assume when discussing the sampling from two populations that only *equal* sample sizes from each are considered.

3.2 Comparing two proportions

This case deals with comparing two proportions. We will choose the sample sizes to control the two types of errors or, in our language, to position the experiment or test at desired Type I and Type II levels. To keep the number of curves included to a reasonable number, and because we can only include one combination of Type I and Type II level on a figure in this case, we have chosen to show curves where the Type I and Type II levels are the same.

Figures 11 through 16 are applicable in this case. As with the previous situation involving proportions, we will need to specify a bound away from one-half that we believe the lower proportion will not cross.

3.2.1 Examples

Suppose that a business's telecommunications coordinator wants to compare the proportion of telephone calls with high noise levels from two interexchange carriers. Suppose that the coordinator wants to have a 90% chance of concluding that two proportions are equal when they indeed are and a similar 90% chance of concluding that they are different when the true proportions differ by 5%. This is a two-sided hypothesis test, which is stated as follows:

$$H_0 : p_1 = p_2 \tag{3.1}$$

$$H_A : \left| p_1 - p_2 \right| = .05.$$

Further suppose that prior evidence leads us to believe that the lower proportion will be no higher than 15%. Since we have specified Type I and Type II levels of 90%, Figure 14 is applicable. Then in Figure 14, for $\Delta = 5$ and an abscissa of 15%, we see that a sample of 1000 calls is needed; that is, a sample of 1000 calls of *each* carrier is necessary.

Now let us compare that with the one-sided example. Suppose we know that $p_1 \leqslant p_2$. We want to be 90% sure of concluding that $p_1 < p_2$ when $p_2 = p_1 + .05$. Thus, the hypothesis test is stated as follows:

$$H_0 : p_1 = p_2 \tag{3.2}$$

$$H_A : p_2 \geqslant p_1 + 0.05.$$

Hence we use Figure 11, and see that a sample size of about 750 is needed, somewhat less than the two-sided case.

3.2.2 Important points

1. If we know that *both* of the proportions are bounded away from one-half by a certain value, then we can use a smaller sample size. In the above two-sided example, if we know that *both* of the proportions are less than 15%, and we want to use $\Delta = 5$, then we will use as the abscissa 10 $(15 - 5)$, and read a sample size of 750 on the $\Delta = 5$ curve in Figure 14. (It is only a coincidence that this number is the same as the answer for the one-sided case example above.)

2. See also "Important points," Section 2.2.2.

3.2.3 Curve equations

Figures 14 through 16, for two-sided tests, are based on the following equation, which is given in Mace (1974):

$$n = 2\left[\frac{Z\left(\frac{1+A}{2}\right) + Z(B)}{\delta}\right]^2 \qquad (3.3)$$

where

$$\delta = 2arcsin\left(\sqrt{\frac{lower\ percent\ +\ \Delta}{100}}\right) - 2arcsin\left(\sqrt{\frac{lower\ percent}{100}}\right) \qquad (3.4)$$

and A is the Type I level, expressed as a proportion, and B is the Type II level expressed as a proportion. By way of comparison, the equation for the one-sided test, in Figures 11 through 13, is given by:

$$n = 2\left[\frac{Z(A)+Z(B)}{\delta}\right]^2. \qquad (3.5)$$

In both the one-sided and two-sided test curves, we have used $A=B$, to minimize the number of curves needed.

3.3 Comparing two rates

This case deals with the comparing of two rates. This case is applicable, for example, in determining whether a design change has improved the failure rate of a product from an earlier vintage or, whether a new type of brakes on an automobile improves the collision rate over an earlier vintage. In this case curves for both one-sided tests (Figures 17 through 19) and two-sided tests (Figures 20 through 22) curves are included. The curves show the number of failures that need to be observed to achieve the desired Type I and Type II error levels.

3.3.1 Example

Suppose that a reliability engineer needs to compare the failure rate, λ_C, of circuit pack C with the failure rate, λ_D, of circuit pack D. The engineer knows that $\lambda_C \geqslant \lambda_D$, and wants to devise a laboratory experiment so that the probability of concluding that λ_C and λ_D are not significantly different when they are, in fact, equal is 0.90, and the probability of rejecting the hypothesis of equality when λ_C is twice λ_D is also 0.90. So we want to position the experiment at both the 90% Type I and the 90% Type II levels. Therefore, the hypothesis test is stated:

$$H_0 : \lambda_C = \lambda_D \qquad (3.6)$$

$$H_A : \lambda_C \geqslant 2 \cdot \lambda_D.$$

This is the one-sided situation, so we use Figure 17 and see that slightly fewer than 30 failures *of each pack* need to be observed in the experiment.

In comparison, let us look at the analogous two-sided example. The engineer does not know in advance which of the two rates is the larger and wants to reject the hypothesis of equality with probability 0.90 when the ratio $\dfrac{\lambda_C}{\lambda_D}$ is either 2 or 0.5. So the hypothesis test is stated:

$$H_0 : \lambda_C = \lambda_D \tag{3.7}$$

$$H_A : \frac{\lambda_C}{\lambda_D} \geqslant 2 \ or \ \frac{\lambda_C}{\lambda_D} \leqslant 0.5.$$

In this case we use Figure 20 and see that the engineer needs to observe approximately 37 failures *of each pack* in the experiment.

3.3.2 Important points

See "Important points," Section 2.3.2.

3.3.3 Curve equations

The two-sided curves are based on the following equation:

$$F = 0.5 \left[\frac{Z(B) + Z\left[\dfrac{1+A}{2}\right]}{\ln\sqrt{R}} \right]^2. \tag{3.8}$$

The one-sided curves are based on the following equation:

$$F = 0.5 \left[\frac{Z(B) + Z(A)}{\ln\sqrt{R}} \right]^2. \tag{3.9}$$

Both equations are given in Mace (1974). A is the Type I level expressed as a proportion, B is the Type II level expressed as a proportion, and R is the ratio (>1) stated in the alternative hypothesis.

3.4 Comparing the means of two normal distributions

This case is applicable, for example, to comparing the average loss in fiber-optic cables resulting from two different splicing techniques or comparing the number of "good" bytes of storage available on floppy disks manufactured by two suppliers.

As in the other comparing cases, we will specify the sample size so that we can position the test/experiment at desired Type I and Type II levels. Figures 23 through 25 deal with the one-sided situation, and Figures 26 through 28 deal with the two-sided situation. The curves are accessed by specifying the Type I level, Type II level, and the ratio of the difference of means (specified in the alternative hypothesis) to the *known common* standard deviation. The means of the two distributions will be denoted as μ_1 and μ_2 and the common standard deviation as σ.

3.4.1 Example

We want to compare two different methods of splicing fiber-optic cable. We are willing to assume that the loss per fiber caused by the splicing is normally distributed for each of the methods, and that the standard deviation is 0.1 dB. When the two methods are, in fact, equal, we want to make the correct conclusion with probability 0.95, and when the difference in the average loss is 0.075 dB, we wish to draw the correct conclusion with probability 0.99. So the required Type I level is 95% and the required Type II level is 99%. The hypothesis test is specified by

$$H_0 : \mu_1 = \mu_2 \tag{3.10}$$

$$H_A : \left| \mu_1 - \mu_2 \right| = 0.075.$$

With Figure 27 we use the 99% curve and an abscissa of $0.75 = (0.075/0.1)$, and see that a sample of 60 splices performed by *each* method is required.

3.4.2 Important points

1. The assumption is made that the two populations have the *same* standard deviation, σ.

2. The curves given here assume that σ is *known*. The procedure for the case in which σ is unknown and must be guessed prior to the experiment or estimated with data requires the use of the noncentral t-distribution. It is difficult to accurately determine quantiles of this distribution. For the reader interested in the case in which σ is *unknown*, there are some useful approximations for the quantiles of the noncentral t-distribution, for example, in Johnson and Kotz (1970).

3. So if σ is *unknown* and these curves are used, the required sample size is *underspecified*. As a rule of thumb, the curves would be be in error by 10% to 20%.

4. See also "Important points," Section 2.4.2.

3.4.3 Curve equations

The one-sided test curves in Figures 23 through 25 are based on the following equation, given in Mace (1974):

$$n = 2 \left[\frac{Z(A) + Z(B)}{\left(\frac{\mu_1 - \mu_2}{\sigma} \right)} \right]^2 . \tag{3.11}$$

The two-sided test curves in Figures 26 through 28 are based on the following equation:

$$n = 2 \left[\frac{Z\left(\frac{1 + A}{2} \right) + Z(B)}{\left(\frac{\mu_1 - \mu_2}{\sigma} \right)} \right]^2 . \tag{3.12}$$

A is the Type I level expressed as a proportion, and B is the Type II level expressed as a proportion.

3.5 Comparing the variances of two normal distributions

This case is applicable, for example, when comparing two manufacturing techniques or designs for their effect on the resulting variation in the distribution of manufactured units. Only one-sided test curves are provided in Figures 29 through 31. The curves are accessed by Type I and Type II levels and the ratio of variances specified in the alternative hypothesis.

3.5.1 Example

A manufacturing engineer needs to compare the variation in dimensions of piece parts from two suppliers. The engineer is currently using supplier 1 in the manufacturing process and is only willing to switch to supplier 2 if the variance in process 2 is half or less than that of process 1. Furthermore, the engineer wants to achieve a Type I level of 0.95 and a Type II level of 0.90. So the hypothesis is specified:

$$H_0 : \sigma_1^2 = \sigma_2^2 \tag{3.13}$$

$$H_A : \sigma_1^2 \geqslant 2\sigma_2^2.$$

Using Figure 30, at an abscissa of 2 and on the 90% curve, we see that a sample of 70 is required. That is, 70 units from *each* process are necessary.

3.5.2 Important points

See "Important points," Section 2.5.2.

3.5.3 Curve equations

The curves in Figures 29 through 31 are based on the following procedure, which is given in Mace (1974). Let

$$n' = 1 + \left[\frac{Z(A) + Z(B)}{\ln(\sqrt{R})} \right]^2.$$

Then through iteration find $n > n'$ so that:

$$F(A, n-1, n-1) = F(B, n-1, n-1) \cdot R, \tag{3.14}$$

where $F(\alpha, m_1, m_2)$ is the α quantile of the F distribution with m_1 and m_2 degrees of freedom. A is the Type I level expressed as a proportion, and B is the Type II level expressed as a proportion.

Hopefully the curves in Figures 29 through 31 are complete enough so that the reader will never have to perform this iteration. The method is included for completeness. One way to carry out the iteration would be to use a simple procedure such as that shown in the flowchart in Section 2.4.3.

4. SELECTING THE BETTER OF TWO PARAMETERS

4.1 Overview of selecting

Selecting is different from comparing in a subtle way. In selecting, we are forced to select one of the parameters as being better in some predefined sense. In comparing, we have the option of accepting the hypothesis that the parameters are equal. We will select the sample size to control the probability of making the correct selection when one parameter is, in fact, better by a specified degree. Because the comparing situation requires control of both the Type I and Type II levels but, in essence, the selecting situation deals only with controlling the Type II levels, the sample sizes for selecting are smaller than the analogous sample sizes for comparing. Another way of looking at the difference between comparing and selecting is that in comparing, we frequently have some prior preference, such as a process or product currently in use; in selecting, we frequently do not have such a preference.

4.2 Selecting the better of two proportions

This case is applicable to choosing which of two manufacturing techniques produces the fewer defective units, which of two drugs causes the higher percentage of patients to be cured, etc. We will agree beforehand that we will select the population whose sampled data are better, in the prescribed sense. We will specify the sample size so that when their true difference is at least Δ, the probability of selecting the correct proportion is B. As in the other cases dealing with proportions, we need to specify a bound away from 50% that the proportion more distant from 50% will not cross. Figures 32 through 35A are applicable in this case.

4.2.1 Example

Suppose we wish to choose between two drugs for treating a certain virus. We wish to have a 90% chance of making the correct choice when the difference in the true percentage of patients cured is 5%. Furthermore, we know that the larger of the two cure percentages is greater than 85%. So in Figure 33, for $\Delta = 5$ and for an abscissa of 15, we see that a sample of 180 is needed. That is, we need a sample of 180 patients treated by each drug, for a total sample of 360. We used the abscissa of 15 because the curves are symmetrical about one half and, therefore, 15 is the applicable abscissa for the 85% bound.

4.2.2 Important points

See "Important points," Section 2.2.2.

4.2.3 Curve equations

The curves in Figures 32 through 35A are based on the following equation, given in Mace (1974):

$$n = 2\left[\frac{Z(B)}{\delta}\right]^2 \tag{4.1}$$

where

$$\delta = 2arcsin\left[\sqrt{\frac{lower\ percent}{100} + \frac{\Delta}{100}}\right] - 2arcsin\left[\sqrt{\frac{lower\ percent}{100}}\right] \tag{4.2}$$

and B is the probability of making the correct selection under the stated conditions.

4.3 Selecting the better of two rates

In this case we will select the better of two rates. We will agree beforehand that we will select the population whose sample data are better, in the prescribed sense. We will select the sample size to assure that if the true ratio of the unknown rates is R, then we will make the correct selection with probability B. The curves in Figure 36 are applicable to this case. The required number of observed failures increases as R decreases toward 1; the closer together the true unknown rates are, the harder it is to distinguish between them.

4.3.1 Example

Suppose that we are interested in selecting one of two integrated circuits for use in a critical part of a system. We want to run a laboratory experiment to determine which has the smaller steady-state failure rate. We want to be 90% certain that we make the correct selection when the larger rate is 1.5 times the smaller. So in Figure 36, for an abscissa of 1.5 and on the 90% curve, we see that 20 failures must be observed in the experiment. That is, 20 failures *of each type of IC* must be observed.

4.3.2 Important points

See "Important points," Section 2.3.2.

4.3.3 Curve equations

The curves in Figure 36 are based on the following equation, which is given in Mace (1974):

$$F = 2 \left[\frac{Z(B)}{\ln R} \right]^2 \qquad (4.3)$$

where B is the probability of making the correct selection if the ratio of the true rates is R.

4.4 Selecting the better mean of two normal distributions

This case is applicable, for example, to choosing which of two fiber-optic splicing techniques should be used to minimize the resulting loss, or which of two print head designs should be used to maximize the number of characters printed before the print head wears out. Our selection will be based on which sample mean is better, and we wish to control the probability that we make the correct decision when the difference in the true population means is a specified proportion of the common standard deviation. Figure 37 shows the number of samples required to achieve the desired probability of making a correct decision. The curves are accessed by the ratio of the difference in the means to the common standard deviation. As this ratio decreases, it is harder to distinguish between the two populations; therefore, a larger sample size is needed.

4.4.1 Example

A telephone company wants to select one of two fiber-optic splicing techniques. Past data indicate that loss resulting from each technique follows a normal distribution with a standard deviation of 0.5 dB per fiber. The company wants to structure a test so that the probability of selecting the better technique is 99% when one has an average loss of 0.2 dB less than the other. So in Figure 37 and the 99% curve at an abscissa of 0.4 = 0.2/0.5, we see that a sample of just under 70 splices *of each* technique is required.

4.4.2 Important points

1. The assumption needs to be made that the standard deviations of the two populations are the same, albeit unknown.

2. If we are to err in the prior estimate of σ, we should err on the larger side.

3. See also "Important points," Section 2.4.2.

4.4.3 Curve equations

The curves in Figure 37 are based on the following procedure, given in Mace (1974):

$$n' = 2\left[\frac{Z(B)}{(\mu_1 - \mu_2)/\sigma'}\right]^2. \tag{4.4}$$

Then a value $n > n'$ is found for which:

$$n = 2\left[\frac{t(n-1,B)}{(\mu_1 - \mu_2)/\sigma'}\right]^2 \tag{4.5}$$

where $t(m, \alpha)$ is the α quantile of the central t-distribution with m degrees of freedom, σ' is a prior estimate of the standard deviation, and B is the probability of making the correct selection when the means are μ_1 and μ_2.

4.5 Selecting the better variance of two normal distributions

This case is applicable, for example, to selecting which of two processes or designs minimizes the variation in manufactured products. We want to control the probability of making the correct selection when the ratio of the larger to the smaller true variance is a specified value. We agree beforehand to select the population whose sample variance is better in the predefined sense. Figure 38 is used in this case, and is accessed by the specified ratio of variances. As this ratio decreases toward 1.0, it is harder to distinguish between the two variances, and a larger sample size is needed.

4.5.1 Example

A manufacturing engineer needs to select one of two suppliers who can provide a certain piece part. The engineer wants to choose the supplier with the least variation in a critical dimension, which is assumed to follow a normal distribution. The engineer will pick the supplier whose sample variance is smaller, and wants to be 95% certain of making the correct selection when the true ratio of the variances is 2.0. So in Figure 38, on the 95% curve, we see that a sample of about 25 is necessary; that is, 25 parts from *each* supplier are required.

4.5.2 Important points

See "Important points," Section 2.5.2.

4.5.3 Curve equations

The curves in Figure 38 are based upon the following equation, which is given in Mace (1974):

$$n = 1 + 4\left[\frac{Z(B)}{\ln(R)}\right]^2 \tag{4.6}$$

where B is the probability of making the correct selection when the ratio of the true variances is R.

5. TESTING A HYPOTHESIS ABOUT ONE PARAMETER

5.1 Overview of hypothesis testing

In testing a hypothesis about one parameter, we will select the sample size to control the two kinds of errors that can be made.

		TRUTH	
		Null Hypothesis true	Null Hypothesis false
ACTION	Accept Null Hypothesis	No error	Type II error
	Reject Null Hypothesis	Type I error	No error

As the above table illustrates, we can make two kinds of errors. As in the comparing case, we will use the terminology Type I level and Type II level, for consistency with other cases. For example, when the Type I error is 5% or less, we will say that we are at the 95% Type I level, and similarly for Type II level. To specify the sample size, we will need to specify a more exact situation than "null hypothesis false." For example, we might specify some exact value of the parameter which is inconsistent with the null hypothesis.

We also need to make the distinction here between one-sided and two-sided tests. If we specify the null hypothesis in the form $X = x$, then we would reject this hypothesis if the true value of X is distant from x *on either side*; thus, this is a two-sided test. If, on the other hand, we specify the null hypothesis in the form $X \leqslant x$, then we would want to reject the null hypothesis if X is somewhat larger then x; this is a one-sided test. In accordance with my experience in reliability and quality assurance problems, I have included one-sided test curves for all four parametric situations but the two-sided test curves only for the normal mean. For the reader interested in other two-sided tests, the topic is covered in Chapter 6 of Mace (1974).

5.2 Testing a hypothesis about one proportion

Here we will deal with one-sided tests only, because they are much more frequently used for proportions than two-sided tests. For example, we are more likely to formulate a null hypothesis that the percent defective of a manufacturing process is less than or equal to some value, rather than exactly equal to some value. We wish to test the hypothesis that a proportion is less than or equal to Φ_0. We will look at a sample of n units.

    a.   If we observe in the sample that a number of units less than or equal to c, the acceptance number, has the trait associated with the proportion, then we accept the hypothesis that the proportion is less than or equal to Φ_0.

    b.   If we observe that more than c of the units have the trait, then we reject the hypothesis in favor of the alternative that the proportion is greater than Φ_0.

We wish to structure the test so that if the true value of the proportion is Φ_0, we will terminate in (a) with probability A, and if the true value of the proportion is Φ_1, we will terminate in (b) with probability B. The quantity $1-A$ is usually called the probability of a Type I error; the quantity $1-B$ is usually called the probability of a Type II error. This is, of course, a well-known problem in acceptance sampling where the correspondence is as shown below:

(a)	Lot accepted	
(b)	Lot rejected	
n	Sample size	
c	Acceptance number	
Φ_0	AQL	(5.1)
Φ_1	LTPD	
Probability of Type I error	Producer's risk	
Probability of Type II error	Consumer's risk	

Figures 39, 41, 43, and 45 give the sample sizes for this case for values of Φ_0 equal to 1%, 2%, 5%, and 10%, respectively. Figures 40, 42, 44, and 46 give the corresponding acceptance numbers.

5.2.1 Example

Suppose that we want to have a sampling plan for which the producer's and consumer's risk are both 0.05, the AQL is 1%, and the LTPD is 5%. In Figure 39, for an abscissa of 5, on the 90% curve, we see that a sample of just over 100 is needed.

5.2.2 Curve equations

The curves in Figures 39, 41, 43, and 45 are based on the following equation, which is given in Mace (1974):

$$n = \left[\frac{Z(A) + Z(B)}{2 \cdot arcsin\sqrt{\Phi_0} - 2 \cdot arcsin\sqrt{\Phi_1}} \right]^2 . \qquad (5.2)$$

But because we used $A = B$ in constructing the curves, this reduces to:

$$n = \left[\frac{Z(A)}{arcsin\sqrt{\Phi_0} - arcsin\sqrt{\Phi_1}} \right]^2 . \qquad (5.3)$$

The acceptance number curves given in Figures 40, 42, 44, and 46 are based on the following equation, which is derived from the results of Mace (1974):

$$c = n \cdot sin^2 \left\{ arcsin(\sqrt{\Phi_0}) + \frac{Z(A)}{2\sqrt{n}} \right\} \qquad (5.4)$$

A is the Type I level expressed as a proportion, and B is the Type II level expressed as a proportion.

5.3 Testing a hypothesis about one rate

In this case we discuss one-sided tests only, because they occur more frequently than the two-sided tests in reliability and quality assurance problems. We wish to test the hypothesis that a failure rate is less than or equal to a specified value, V. Based on the data we observe, we will either

a. Accept the hypothesis that the failure rate is less than or equal to V, or
b. Reject the above hypothesis in favor of the alternative that the failure rate is greater than V.

We wish to structure the test so that if the true value of the failure rate is V, we make decision (a) with probability A and if the true value of the failure rate is $R \cdot V$, we make decision (b) with probability B. Note that $R > 1$. Figures 47 through 49 show the number of failures that need to be observed to achieve the desired Type I and Type II levels.

5.3.1 Example

Suppose we wish to test the hypothesis that the rate at which automobiles cross a certain point on a highway is Λ per hour or less. If the true rate is 1.4Λ, we want to be 99% certain that we reject the hypothesis; if the true rate is Λ, we want to be 99% certain to accept the hypothesis. From Figure 49, at an abscissa of 1.4 and on the 99% curve, we see that we need to observe 190 cars passing the point on the highway.

5.3.2 Important points

See "Important points," Section 2.3.2.

5.3.3 Curve equations

The curves in Figures 47 through 49 are based on the following equation, which is given in Mace (1974):

$$F = 0.25 \left[\frac{Z(A) + Z(B)\sqrt{R}}{1 - \sqrt{R}} \right]^2 . \tag{5.5}$$

When we use $A = B$, this reduces to:

$$F = 0.25 \left[\frac{Z(A)\left[1 + \sqrt{R}\right]}{1 - \sqrt{R}} \right]^2 . \tag{5.6}$$

A is the Type I level expressed as a proportion, and B is the Type II level expressed as a proportion.

5.4 Testing a hypothesis about the mean of a normal distribution

This case is applicable to determining if the average resistance value of a population of resistors has some specified value, or if the average amount of soda put in bottles in a bottling factory exceeds some amount. Since this situation typically is applied to both one-sided and two-sided problems, the curves for both are included. Figures 50 through 52 cover the one-sided case and Figures 53 through 55 cover the two-sided case. In the one-sided test, for example, we will either

a. Accept the hypothesis that the mean, μ, is greater than or equal to μ_0, or

b. Reject the above hypothesis in favor of the alternative that the mean is less than μ_0 and is, in fact, equal to μ_1.

We will select the sample size to achieve specified Type I and Type II levels. The curves are accessed by the ratio $\dfrac{\mu_1 - \mu_0}{\sigma}$, where σ is the standard deviation.

5.4.1 Example

Suppose we want to determine if a bottling factory is meeting the requirements for putting at least a certain amount of soda in bottles. Suppose that we are willing to assume that the distribution of the amount put in the bottles follows a normal distribution with known standard deviation of 0.5 ounce. The requirement is that the bottles contain at least 16 ounces of soda. We want to have a 90% Type I level test, and we want to have a 99% Type II level test for the alternative of 15.75

ounces. So the hypotheses are:

$$H_0 : \mu \geqslant 16.00 \qquad (5.7)$$

$$H_A : \mu = 15.75$$

Then in Figure 50, on the 99% curve and for an abscissa of $0.5 = \dfrac{16 - 15.75}{0.5}$, we see that a sample of 55 bottles is required.

5.4.2 Important points

1. Exact calculation of curves applicable when the standard deviation is *unknown* requires use of the noncentral *t*-distribution. It is difficult to accurately determine quantiles of this distribution. The approximate curves given in Figures 50 through 55 are applicable for the case when the standard deviation is *known*. For the case when the standard deviation is *unknown* and σ' is merely an a priori estimate, the curves *under* specify the sample size required.

2. See also "Important points," Section 2.4.2.

5.4.3 Curve equations

The one-sided test curves given in Figures 50 through 52 are based on the following equation, which is given in Mace (1974):

$$n = \left[\frac{Z(A) + Z(B)}{(\mu_0 - \mu_1)/\sigma'} \right]^2 . \qquad (5.8)$$

The two-sided test curves given in Figures 53 through 55 are based on the following equation, which is given in Mace (1974):

$$n = \left[\frac{Z\left(\dfrac{1+A}{2}\right) + Z(B)}{(\mu_0 - \mu_1)/\sigma'} \right]^2 . \qquad (5.9)$$

A is the Type I level expressed as a proportion and B is the Type II level expressed as a proportion.

5.5 Testing a hypothesis about the variance of a normal distribution

This case is applicable, for example, to testing whether the variation in a manufacturing process is less than a specified amount. Figures 56 through 58 give curves for this case. The curves are accessed by the ratio of the variances specified in the null and alternative hypothesis. The sample sizes are selected to achieve specified Type I and Type II levels, similar to other cases in this chapter.

5.5.1 Example

Suppose that a manufacturing engineer needs to test the hypothesis that the variance of the population of lengths of car doors is 0.25 cm^2 or less. The engineer assumes that the construction process is such that these lengths are normally distributed and wants to construct a test so that the probability of rejecting the hypothesis is 0.10 when the true variance is 0.25 cm^2, and the probability of rejecting the hypothesis is 0.90 when the true variance is 0.36 cm^2.

The hypotheses are

$$H_0 : \sigma^2 \leqslant 0.25 \tag{5.10}$$

$$H_A : \sigma^2 = 0.36 .$$

So this test will be at the 90% Type I and Type II levels. We see in Figure 56, on the 90% curve and an abscissa of $1.44 = 0.36/0.25$, that a sample of 100 is needed.

5.5.2 Important points

See "Important points," Section 2.5.2.

5.5.3 Curve equations

The curves are based upon the following procedure given in Mace (1974). First determine an initial approximation

$$n' = 1.5 + 0.5 \cdot \left[\frac{Z(A) + R \cdot Z(B)}{R - 1} \right]^2 . \tag{5.11}$$

Then find $n > n'$ which satisfies

$$\chi^2(1-A;n-1) = R^2 \chi^2(B;n-1) \tag{5.12}$$

where $\chi^2(\alpha,m)$ is the α quantile of the chi-square distribution with m degrees of freedom, A is the Type I level expressed as a proportion, and B is the Type II level expressed as a proportion.

6. CONSTRUCTING TOLERANCE INTERVALS

6.1 Overview of tolerance intervals

This chapter deals with the construction of tolerance intervals. A tolerance interval is an interval that is constructed from sample data to contain a specified proportion of the population with a high degree of confidence. Tolerance intervals can be one sided or two sided. For example, if the population of interest has as its ranges all real numbers, both positive and negative, then one-sided intervals would have the form $(-\infty, U)$ or (L, ∞), whereas the two-sided intervals would have the form (L, U). Alternatively one-sided intervals can be expressed as "L or more," "at least L," "U or less," or in other equivalent terms.

While a tolerance interval might seem equivalent to a confidence interval, it most assuredly is *not*. As was discussed in Chapter 2, a confidence interval is an interval for a *parameter* of a population, whereas the tolerance interval is an interval for *members* of the population itself. Hahn (1970a, 1970b) gives a good discussion of the differences between confidence intervals, tolerance intervals, and another type of interval not discussed in this text, prediction intervals.

As an example, we might want to construct a tolerance interval so that the interval contains 95% of the population with probability 0.90. One frequent application of the use of tolerance intervals is in the area of "capacity" problems. Suppose a metropolitan transportation company needs to know how many subway cars are needed to adequately handle passengers on a single line. The observed data will take the form of the number of cars that would have been adequate to sufficiently handle the passengers during a sampled day. The company sets as its objective the ability to sufficiently handle passengers on 95% of the days. This means that it wants to construct a 95% one-sided tolerance interval, since it is interested in having *at least as many* cars as are needed on 95% of the days. Similar capacity problems might deal with call-handling capabilities of a communications network, hot-water capacity of a boiler, vehicular traffic capacity of a highway, and so forth.

We use the approach of Kirkpatrick (1977) in this text. We will select a sample size so that:

a. The probability is A that the interval contains between $P - \Delta$ and $P + \Delta$ of the population;

b. The probability is $(1 + A)/2$ that the interval contains *at least* $P - \Delta$ of the population; and

c. The probability is $(1 - A)/2$ that the interval contains *more than* $P + \Delta$ of the population.

We will refer to A as the confidence level, P as the population proportion, and Δ as the population increment.

6.2 Nonparametric case

In this situation we do not know what the underlying distribution is, and we are unwilling to make any assumptions about it; so this is called the nonparametric case. Figures 59 through 61 are appropriate for this situation. The curves are accessed by the population proportion (P), the confidence level (A), and the population proportion increment (Δ). The theory used specifies the same sample size for one and two-sided cases. All three of P, A, and Δ are proportions in the range 0 to 1.

6.2.1 Example

Suppose we want to construct a tolerance interval for use in constructing a hot-water boiler for a manufacturing facility. We want to be able to adequately handle the needs of the plant on 95% of the days. So the question we might ask is: How many days of hot water usage should we sample so that we can construct a 0.95 population proportion interval, with 0.02 population increment, at the

90% confidence level. In Figure 60, on the 90% curve at an abscissa of 0.02, we see that approximately 325 days must be sampled.

6.2.2 Important points

1. Obviously, $P + \Delta$ must not exceed 1.0, and the curves reflect that.

2. The irregularities in the curves are caused by imperfections in the numerical analysis software. So here the warning given in Section 1.4 needs to be repeated: these curves are only approximations to be used for general guidelines.

6.2.3 Curve equations

The curves in Figures 59 through 61 are based on finding values of m and n that satisfy the following equations given by Kirkpatrick (1977):

$$\frac{1 - A}{2} \geqslant 1 - \sum_{i=0}^{m-2} \binom{n}{i} (1 - P - \Delta)^i (P + \Delta)^{n-i} \tag{6.1}$$

$$\frac{1 - A}{2} \geqslant 1 - \sum_{i=0}^{m-1} \binom{n}{i} (1 - P + \Delta)^i (P - \Delta)^{n-i} \tag{6.2}$$

where n is the sample size and m defines the order statistic used in constructing the tolerance interval.

6.3 Normal distribution

Here we assume that the underlying distribution is normal. Two-sided tolerance intervals would then take the form $\bar{x} \pm ks$, where $\bar{x}$ is the sample average and s is the sample standard deviation. Kirkpatrick's (1977) method specifies different sample sizes for one- and two-sided cases, but because the results are roughly the same (usually only 5% to 10% apart), only one set of curves has been included; these are Figures 62 through 64. With the exception of the distributional assumption, all notation and concepts are the same as in the nonparametric case.

6.3.1 Example

Consider the same example as in Section 6.2.1, but assume that the normal distribution is appropriate. Then in Figure 63, on the 90% curve at an abscissa of 0.02, we see that a sample size of about 160 needs to be taken. Notice how much smaller this is than the sample for the nonparametric case (325). The additional information (or assumption) that the normal distribution is appropriate cuts the required sample size in half.

6.3.2 Important points

See "Important points," Section 6.2.2.

6.3.3 Curve equations

The curves in Figures 62 through 64 are based on the following equations, which are simplified forms of those given by Kirkpatrick (1977) for the one-sided case:

$$k = \frac{Z(P + \Delta) + Z(P - \Delta)}{2} \tag{6.3}$$

$$n = 4\left[1 + \frac{k^2}{2}\right] \cdot \left[\frac{Z\left(\frac{1 + A}{2}\right)}{Z(P + \Delta) - Z(P - \Delta)}\right]^2 . \tag{6.4}$$

7. INCORPORATING ECONOMICS OF SAMPLING

7.1 Overview of approach

The considerations in the previous chapters caused sample sizes to be chosen to control the risk of making certain kinds of errors. In this chapter we will pick the sample sizes to minimize the sum of two costs: the cost of doing the sample and the cost involved with having less than perfect information on which to make a decision. The cost of sampling increases with the sample size, while the cost associated with imperfect information decreases. The trick is to pick the sample size that balances these two considerations by minimizing the total cost. This concept has been discussed frequently in the published literature, for example, Lee (1981); Wayne and Grimm (1983); and Noz, Redding, and Ware (1983). It is illustrated in Figure 65. The cost-of-sampling curve (1) is typically linear, and is often of the form $K + c \cdot n$, where n is the sample size. The curve (2) describing the cost of imperfect information usually falls rapidly for small values of sample size, then tends to level off due to the decreased incremental utility of additional samples. The total cost curve (3) is typically flat near the minimum value. That means that picking a sample a little more or a little less than the optimum value does not change the total cost very much. All of the theory in this chapter is in Mace (1974), Chapter 11.

7.2 Estimating normal mean: squared error loss

The first case to which we will apply this method is estimating the mean of a normal distribution. The loss we will suffer (or equivalently, the cost we must bear) for using the sample mean $\overline{x}$ as an estimate when the true mean is assumed to be μ is

$$c_1 \cdot (\mu - \overline{x})^2. \tag{7.1}$$

Denote the "fixed" and "variable" costs of sampling by c_2 and c_3, respectively. Then the cost of sampling is a linear function of the sample size, n:

$$c_2 + c_3 n. \tag{7.2}$$

The total cost function is

$$c_1 E[(\mu - \overline{x})^2] + c_2 + c_3 n. \tag{7.3}$$

E is the expectation operator; since $\overline{x}$ can take on many values, we need to take the average of the squared error term. The above equation reduces to

$$\frac{c_1 \sigma^2}{n} + c_2 + c_3 n. \tag{7.4}$$

The value of n that minimizes this function is

$$n = \sigma \sqrt{\frac{c_1}{c_3}}. \tag{7.5}$$

Figure 66 gives curves for this equation for a reasonable range of the parameters. The "Cost Ratio" is $\dfrac{c_1}{c_3}$.

7.2.1 Example

Suppose we are interested in measuring the concentration of a certain chemical in a commercial cleaning formula. We are willing to assume that the concentration from bottle to bottle follows a normal distribution with a standard deviation of 30 parts per million. When our estimate deviates from the truth, we suffer a penalty of $1000 times the square of the difference between the truth and the estimate. The set-up cost for the measurement experiment is $500, and the incremental cost of measuring each bottle is $100. How many bottles of formula should be measured to minimize the total cost?

The cost ratio is $1000/$100 $=$ 10, and $\sigma^2 = 900$. So in Figure 66 we see that just under 100 bottles should be measured.

7.2.2 Important points

Whether or not the variable of interest is normally distributed, the mean of n independent identically distributed random variables will approach a normal distribution as n becomes large. So at least for large sample sizes, the determination of the appropriate sample sizes is insensitive to departures from normality.

7.3 Estimating normal mean: absolute deviation loss

This case is the same as the preceding case, with the exception that the loss due to imperfect information is proportional to the absolute deviation between the truth and the estimate, as opposed to the squared error. Thus the loss is of the form

$$c_1 \left| \mu - \bar{x} \right| . \tag{7.6}$$

So the total cost curve is

$$c_2 + c_3 \cdot n + c_1 \cdot E\left[\left| \mu - \bar{x} \right| \right] . \tag{7.7}$$

Assuming normality, this is equal to

$$c_2 + c_3 \cdot n + c_1 \sigma \sqrt{\frac{2}{\pi n}} . \tag{7.8}$$

The value of n that minimizes total cost is

$$n = 0.5419 \left[\frac{c_1}{c_3} \sigma \right]^{\frac{2}{3}} . \tag{7.9}$$

Figure 67 gives curves for this equation. The "cost ratio" is $\dfrac{c_1}{c_3}$.

7.3.1 Example

Let's continue with the same example as in Section 7.2.1. The cost ratio is still the same, 10, and σ^2 is 900. In Figure 67 we see that a sample of about 23 bottles needs to be measured, which is considerably fewer than when the loss was proportional to the square of the estimation error.

7.3.2 Important points

See "Important points," Section 7.2.2.

7.4 Selecting the better of two normal means

In this case we have independent normal distributions with means μ_1 and μ_2 and a common known variance σ^2. We wish to pick the population with the larger mean. (The results would apply equally well if we wanted to pick the smaller mean.) We will select the population from which the sample mean $\bar{x}$ is the larger. If we pick the correct population, we suffer no penalty. If we pick the wrong population, we suffer a loss that is proportional to the difference between the two true means. Again the sampling cost will be linear.

Suppose that $\mu_1 \geqslant \mu_2$. Then the total cost curve will be

$$p \cdot c_1 (\mu_1 - \mu_2) + c_2 + c_3 \cdot n \qquad (7.10)$$

where p is the probability that $\bar{x}_2$ is greater than $\bar{x}_1$, and n is the sample size. The value of n that minimizes the maximum loss is

$$n = 0.2435 \left[\frac{c_1 \sigma}{c_3} \right]^{\frac{2}{3}}. \qquad (7.11)$$

Figure 68 gives curves for this equation. The cost ratio is $\dfrac{c_1}{c_3}$.

7.4.1 Example

Suppose a manufacturing engineer must decide which of two suppliers of a certain piece part to use for the coming year. The engineer wants to pick the piece part that has the ability to withstand the larger twisting tension force without breaking, and he knows from the projected production figures that every foot pound of decrease in the breaking point will cause the company to incur $10,000 in product repair costs during the next year. The cost of doing an experiment involves a setup cost of $1000 and a cost per unit of $200, because each unit must be destroyed by twisting it until it breaks. In addition, past experience with suppliers of these parts indicates that it is reasonable to assume that the variance of the populations is 3000. Then in Figure 68, for the $\sigma^2 = 3000$ curve and an abscissa of 50, we see that a sample of about 45 must be taken; that is, a sample of 45 *from each supplier*.

7.4.2 Important points

See "Important points," Section 7.2.2.

7.5 Selecting the better of two proportions

Here we wish to pick the better of two proportions. In the following discussion, we will assume that "better" means "smaller"; however, the results would hold equally well if "larger" were substituted. We have two proportions P_1 and P_2, and assume that $P_1 < P_2$. We will select the proportion from whose sample the observed proportion is the smaller. The loss we will incur if we pick P_2, the incorrect choice, is $c_1 (P_2 - P_1)$. If we make the correct choice, we suffer no penalty. The sampling cost is assumed to be linear. If we let $\gamma = (P_1 + P_2 - 1)^2$, and p be the probability of making the incorrect decision, then the total cost curve is

$$c_1 p (P_2 - P_1) + c_2 + c_3 \cdot n. \qquad (7.12)$$

The sample size that minimizes the maximum loss is

$$n = 0.1534 \left[\frac{c_1 \sqrt{1 - \gamma}}{c_3} \right]^{\frac{2}{3}}, \qquad (7.13)$$

where γ is based on any prior information we may have about the two populations. It should be used to bound the sample size. Note that when there is no prior knowledge about the two proportions that would enable one to establish a bound on γ, then we use the value of $\gamma = 0$, which produces the largest sample size.

7.5.1 Example

Suppose a manufacturing engineer must choose one of two suppliers of a certain piece part to use for the next year. The engineer knows that every 1% increase in the percent defective of the piece part will cost the company \$100,000 in product repair costs during the next year. The engineer has estimated that the cost of a sampling experiment will be \$350 to set up the machinery, and \$20 to test each piece. Past experience with the two suppliers makes it reasonable to assume that both P_1 and P_2 are less than .11. This translates into $\gamma > .78^2 \approx .6$ So in Figure 69 on the $\gamma = .6$ curve, at an abscissa of $5000 = 100,000/20$, we see that a sample of approximately 32 should be taken *of each supplier's part*. Note that if we did not have any prior experience with the two suppliers, then the value of $\gamma = 0$ would have to be used, and the sample size would be 42.

7.5.2 Important points

This procedure depends on the normal approximation to the binomial, and is therefore not very accurate in general for small sample sizes. However, for the case in which $\gamma = 0$ is used, the procedure is accurate even for small sample sizes (Somerville [1957]).

7.6 Testing a hypothesis about a normal mean

This case deals with a one-sided test about the mean of a normal distribution. The loss function is broken into two parts, as a function of the true but unknown mean, μ.

1. The loss when we accept the hypothesis is

$$c_1 + c_2\mu . \tag{7.14}$$

2. The loss when we reject the hypothesis is

$$c_3 + c_4\mu . \tag{7.15}$$

The "break-even" value is that value of the mean for which the two components of the loss function are the same, so it does not matter whether we accept or reject the hypothesis. This value is easily seen to be

$$\mu_0 = \frac{c_1 - c_3}{c_4 - c_2} . \tag{7.16}$$

So the hypothesis is formulated

$$H_0 : \mu \geqslant \mu_0 \tag{7.17}$$

$$H_A : \mu < \mu_0 .$$

We will reject the hypothesis if $\bar{x} < \mu_0$ and accept the hypothesis otherwise. The cost of sampling is

$$c_5 + c_6 \cdot n . \tag{7.18}$$

The sample size that minimizes the maximum loss is

$$n = 0.1933 \left[\frac{c_4 - c_2}{c_6}\sigma \right]^{2/3} . \tag{7.19}$$

Figure 70 gives the curves for this case. The "cost ratio" is $\dfrac{c_4 - c_2}{c_6}$.

7.6.1 Example

Suppose that we wish to test a hypothesis that the concentration of a certain chemical in a commercial cleaning formula is less than 200 parts per million. We are willing to assume that the concentration from bottle to bottle follows a normal distribution with standard deviation 30 parts per million. The cost of taking data is $1500 for setting up the experiment and $20 for testing each bottle. If we accept the hypothesis, we will suffer a cost of $1000 per part per million due to product liability costs during the next year. If we reject the hypothesis, we will suffer a cost of $200,000 to throw away the product and redesign the chemical process. So the relevant costs are:

c_1	0
c_2	$1000
c_3	$200,000
c_4	0
c_5	$1500
c_6	$20
cost ratio	50

Since we are testing the hypothesis that the mean is *less* than a standard, and the procedure explained in Section 7.6 assumed that we were testing a hypothesis that the mean is *greater* than a standard, the actual calculated cost ratio was negative. We just use the absolute value in accessing the curves. So in Figure 70, for an abscissa of 50 and a variance of 900, we see that a sample size of about 25 is necessary.

7.6.2 Important points

See "Important points," Section 7.2.2.

7.7 Testing a hypothesis about a proportion

This is similar to the previous case, except now we are dealing with a proportion. We want to do a one-sided test that a proportion is less than or equal to a certain standard value. Again the loss function is divided into two parts

1. The loss associated with accepting the hypothesis is

$$c_1 + c_2 P .$$ (7.20)

2. The loss associated with rejecting the hypothesis is

$$c_3 + c_4 P .$$ (7.21)

The sampling cost is

$$c_5 + c_6 \cdot n .$$ (7.22)

When the true unknown proportion, P, is at the standard value, P_0, the two losses are equal, and it does not matter whether we accept or reject the hypothesis. P_0 is easily seen to be:

$$P_0 = \frac{c_1 - c_3}{c_4 - c_2} .$$ (7.23)

The hypotheses are

$$H_0 : P \leqslant P_0$$ (7.24)

$$H_A : P > P_0 .$$

The null hypothesis is accepted if the sample proportion is less than or equal to P_0 and rejected otherwise. The sample size that minimizes the maximum expected loss is

$$n = 0.1933 \left[\frac{c_2 - c_4}{c_6} \right]^{2/3} \left[P_0 (1 - P_0) \right]^{1/3}. \qquad (7.25)$$

Figure 71 gives the curves for this case. The "cost ratio" is $\dfrac{c_2 - c_4}{c_6}$.

7.7.1 Example

A manufacturer of printed wiring boards must select a sampling plan for deciding whether or not to accept a lot of boards for sending on to a customer. There are 1000 boards in the lot. For every defective board that gets into the hands of the customer, the manufacturer suffers a loss of \$485 due to shipping costs, loss of good will and future business, etc. When the lot is rejected, the manufacturer suffers a loss of \$15,000 − \$15,000 P; notice that if quality is 100% defective, then the loss of rejection is 0. Furthermore, it costs \$50 to inspect each board. So the relevant costs are

c_1	0
c_2	\$485,000
c_3	\$15,000
c_4	-\$15,000
c_5	0
c_6	\$50
cost ratio	\$10,000

P_0 is then 0.03. So in Figure 71 at an abscissa of 10,000 between the curves for $P_0 = 0.02$ and for $P_0 = 0.05$, we see that a sample of about 26 is needed. So the lot would be rejected if more than 26 × 0.03 defects are observed in the sample; that is, one defect would cause the lot to be rejected.

7.7.2 Important points

1. This procedure is based upon the normal approximation to the binomial, and is therefore valid only for sufficiently large sample sizes.

2. For problems similar to the example, the finite population correction can be ignored, only for large lot sizes, as it was here.

7.8 Other economic optimization models

7.8.1 Feedback model of quality behavior

The cost model used in the previous section models the effect of the rejected lot through the savings involved in prohibiting defective product from getting to the customer in that one lot. Another approach to the economics of sampling in quality assurance applications is the feedback model of quality behavior developed by Hoadley (1981). This approach assumes that quality can be in one of two states: "good" and "bad." The quality moves from the good state to the bad with probability P from one unit of time period to the next (for example, the amount of time it takes to produce the next lot). The quality moves from the bad state to the good state with probability d, where d is the detection power of the sample; this is the case because it is assumed that detection of the problem causes the supplier to fix the problem. So the loss function associated with the imperfect information is the weighted average of the costs associated with the two states of quality, where the weights are the proportion of time the quality stays in each state. This original Hoadley model has evolved into the BELLCORE-STD family of economically optimum sampling plans (Brush [1986] and Brush et al. [1984]). These plans address questions such as what fraction of lots to skip while doing skip lot inspection, what sample should be taken from an individual lot, how frequently to perform an audit, and so on.

7.8.2 Price adjusted sampling

Another type of economic sampling deals with the assumption that there is a tradeoff between quality and the price a consumer pays for the product. Through this method, indifference curves can be established that show that for proper pricing, the consumer is indifferent to quality. Foster and Perry (1972), and Hailey and Balbirer (1981) are a few of the authors who have addressed this situation.

GLOSSARY

Abscissa. The horizontal coordinate; this can be read off the scale at the *bottom* of the graph.

Confidence level. A confidence interval is said to have confidence level of A if the process by which the interval was constructed, if repeated a large number of times, would include the true, unknown parameter, a proportion A of the time.

Comparing. A statistical procedure in which we have the options of accepting that the two parameters are equal, or concluding that they are different. (Compare with the definition of Selecting.)

One-sided test. A test of hypothesis in which we reject the null hypothesis if the observed data are too distant *in one specified direction* to be consistent with the null hypothesis.

Ordinate. The vertical coordinate; this can be read off the scale on the *left* side of the graph.

Selecting. A statistical procedure in which we must pick one of the two options given. (Compare with the definition of Comparing.)

Two-sided test. A test of hypothesis in which we reject the null hypothesis if the observed data are too distant *in either direction* to be consistent with the null hypothesis.

Type I error. Rejecting the null hypothesis when it is, in fact, true.

Type I level. The Type I level of A is achieved if the probability of making a Type I error is $1-A$ or less.

Type II error. Failing to reject the null hypothesis when the parameter has some specified value inconsistent with the null hypothesis.

Type II level. The Type II level of B is achieved if the probability of making a Type II error is $1-B$ or less.

Z(x). The x quantile of the standard normal distribution.

BIBLIOGRAPHY

Abadeer, W. W. (1986). "A new approach to the parametric case in sampling," *1986 ASQC Quality Congress Transactions,* pp. 721-726.

Brush, G. G. (1984). "What sample size is needed?" *Proceedings of the Quality in Electronics Conference,* pp. 35-41.

Brush, G. G. (1986). "A new standard plan for sampling," *Bell Communications Research EXCHANGE* (September/October): pp. 23-27.

Brush, G. G.; Guyton, D. A.; Hoadley, A. B.; Huston, W. B.; and Senior, R. A. (1984). "BELLCORE-STD-100: an inspection resource allocation plan," *IEEE Global Communications Conference,* pp. 1119-1124.

Faulkenberry, G. D. and Daly, J. C. (1970). "Sample size for tolerance limits on a normal distribution," *Technometrics* 12:813-821.

Faulkenberry, G. D. and Weeks, P. L. (1968)."Sample size determination for tolerance limits," *Technometrics* 10:343-348.

Foster, J. and Perry, L. (1972). "Price adjusted single sampling with linear indifference," *Journal of Quality Technology* 4 (3): 134-144.

Grubbs, F. E. (1949). "On designing single sampling inspection plans," *Annals of Mathematical Statistics* 20 (2): 242-256.

Guenther, W. C. (1971). "On the determination of single sampling attribute plans based upon a linear cost model and a prior distribution," *Technometrics* 13 (3): 483-487.

Guenther, W. C. (1975). "A sample size formula for non-central t-test," *The American Statistician* 29:120-121.

Harris, M.; Horovitz, D. G.; and Mood, A. M. (1948). "On the determination of sample sizes in designing experiments," *Journal of the American Statistical Association* 43:391-402.

Hahn, G. J. (1970a). "Statistical intervals for a normal population, part I," *Journal of Quality Technology* 2 (2): 115-125.

Hahn, G. J. (1970b). "Statistical intervals for a normal population, part II," *Journal of Quality Technology* 2 (4): 195-206.

Hald, A. (1960). "The compound hypergeometric distribution and a system of single sampling inspection plans based on prior distributions and costs," *Technometrics* 2 (3): 275-340.

Hailey, W. A. and Balbirer, S. D. (1981). "Price adjusted sampling with nonlinear indifference," *1981 ASQC Quality Congress Transactions,* pp. 208-212.

Hiering, V. S. and Hooke, J. A. (1978). "Product performance studies: field tracking for station sets," *Bell Laboratories Record* (December), Special QA issue.

Hoadley, A. B. (1981). "The universal sampling plan," *1981 ASQC Quality Congress Transactions,* pp. 80-87.

Johnson, N. L. and Kotz, S. (1970). *Continuous Univariate Distributions,* Boston, Mass: Houghton Mifflin.

Kirkpatrick, R. L. (1977). "Sample sizes to set tolerance limits," *Journal of Quality Technology* 9:6-12.

Lee, D. (1981). "Minimized cost sampling technique," *1981 ASQC Quality Congress Transactions*, pp. 958-963.

Mace, A. E. (1974). *Sample Size Determination,* Huntington, N.Y.: Robert Krieger.

Noz, W. C.; Redding, B. F.; and Ware, P. A. (1983). "The quality manager's job: optimize costs," *1983 ASQC Quality Congress Transactions*, pp. 301-306.

Odeh, R. E. and Fox, M. (1975). *Sample Size Choice,* New York, N.Y.: Marcel Dekker.

Odeh, R. E. and Owen, D. B. (1980). *Tables for Normal Limits, Sampling Plans, & Screening,* New York, N.Y.: Marcel Dekker.

Sobel, M. and Huyett, M. (1957). "Selecting the best one of several binomial populations," *Bell System Technical Journal* 36 (2): 537-576.

Somerville, P. N. (1957). "Optimum sampling in binomial populations," *Journal of the American Statistical Association* 52: 494-502.

Swann, D. W. (1975). "Field study sample sizes for reliability parameter estimates subject to a time constraint," Bell Telephone Laboratories Technical Memorandum.

Tukey, J. W. (1977). *Exploratory Data Analysis*, Reading, Mass.: Addison-Wesley.

Wayne, J. J. and Grimm, A. F. (1983). "Quality costs: we know where we're going. Do you?" *1983 ASQC Quality Congress Transactions*, pp. 457-462.

Wilks, S. S. (1941). "Determination of sample sizes for setting tolerance limits," *Annals of Mathematical Statistics* 12:91-96.

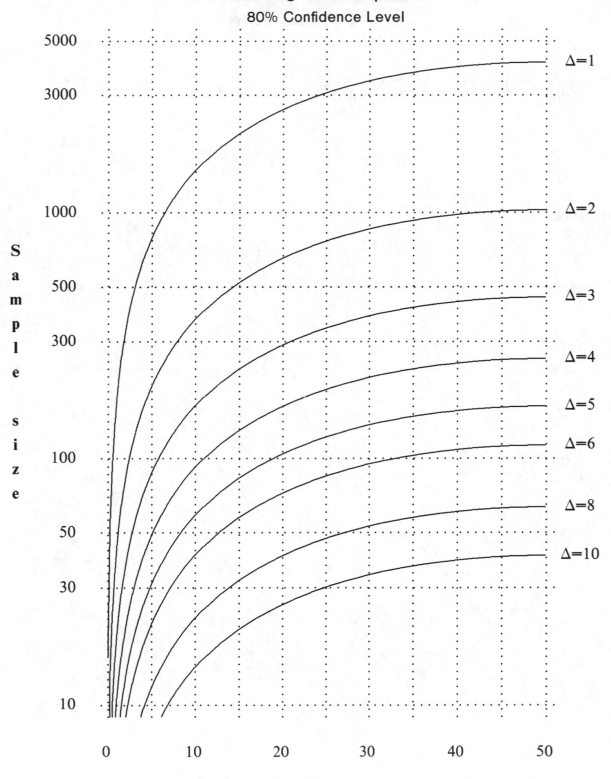

Figure 1

MINIMUM SAMPLE SIZE
Estimating One Proportion
80% Confidence Level

Δ=1

Δ=2

Δ=3

Δ=4

Δ=5

Δ=6

Δ=8

Δ=10

Sample size

Percent

Figure 1A

MINIMUM SAMPLE SIZE
Estimating One Proportion
80% Confidence Level

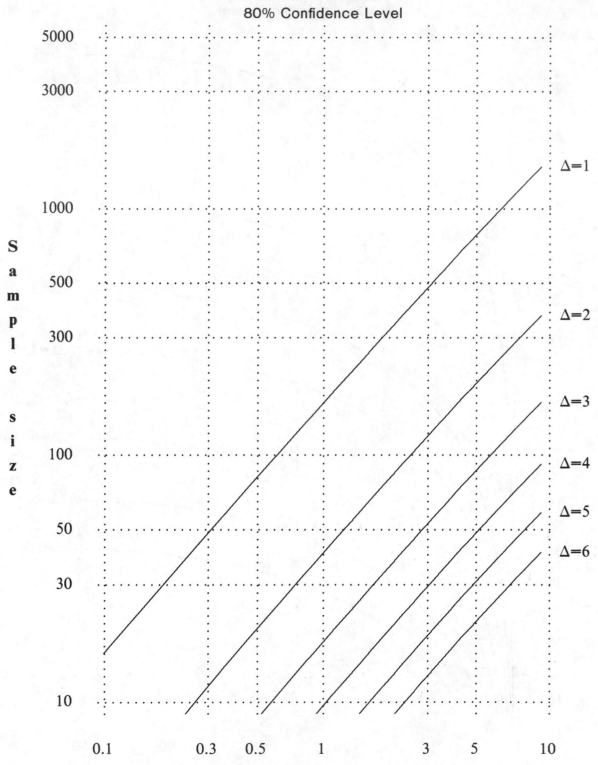

Percent

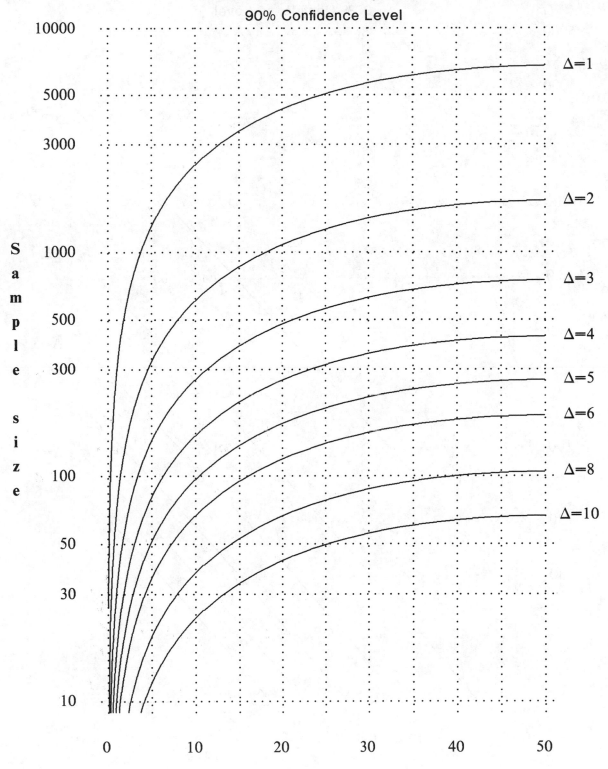

Figure 2

MINIMUM SAMPLE SIZE
Estimating One Proportion
90% Confidence Level

MINIMUM SAMPLE SIZE
Estimating One Proportion
90% Confidence Level

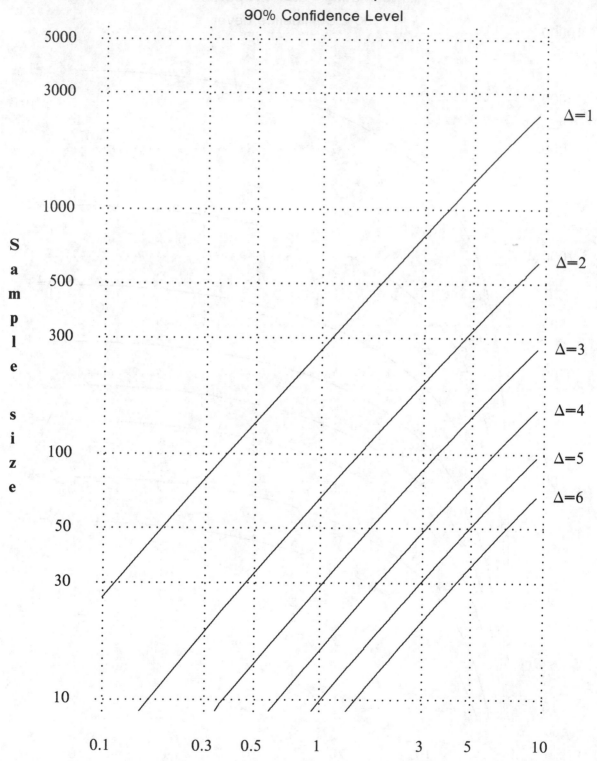

Figure 3

MINIMUM SAMPLE SIZE
Estimating One Proportion
95% Confidence Level

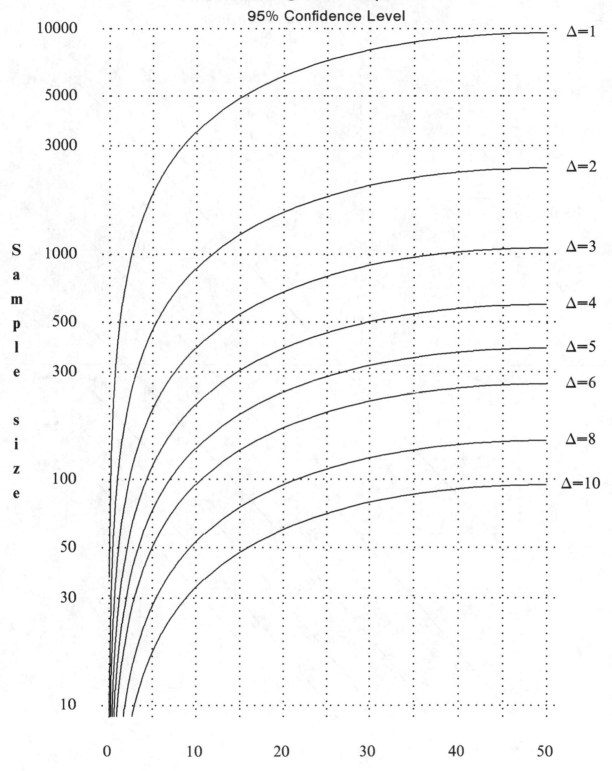

Percent

Figure 3A

MINIMUM SAMPLE SIZE

Estimating One Proportion

95% Confidence Level

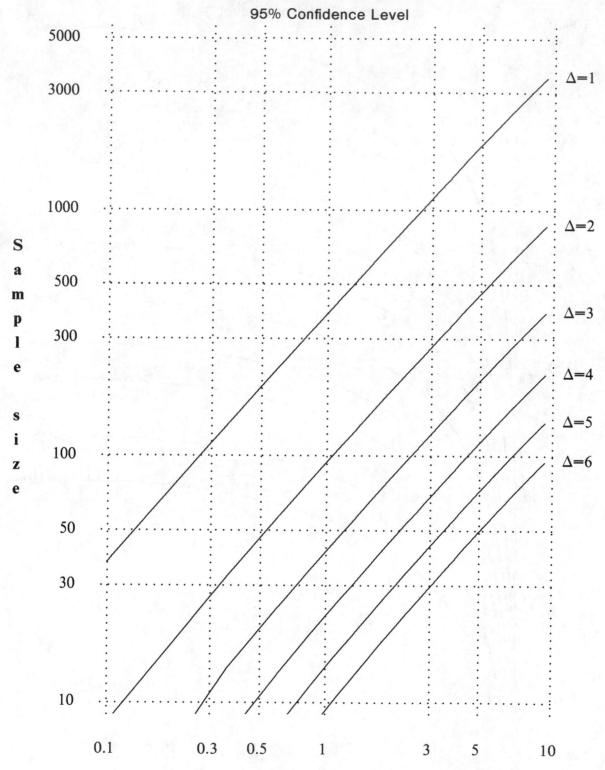

Percent

Figure 4

MINIMUM SAMPLE SIZE
Estimating One Proportion
99% Confidence Level

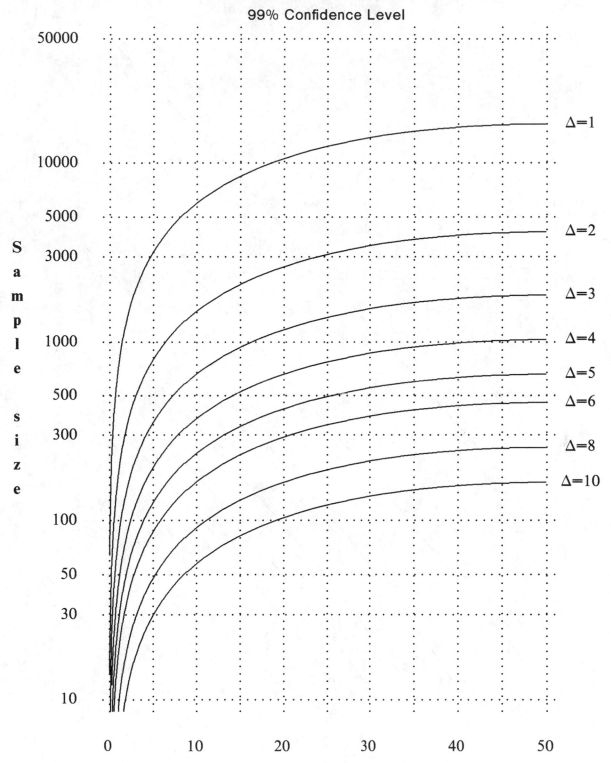

Percent

MINIMUM SAMPLE SIZE
Estimating One Proportion
99% Confidence Level

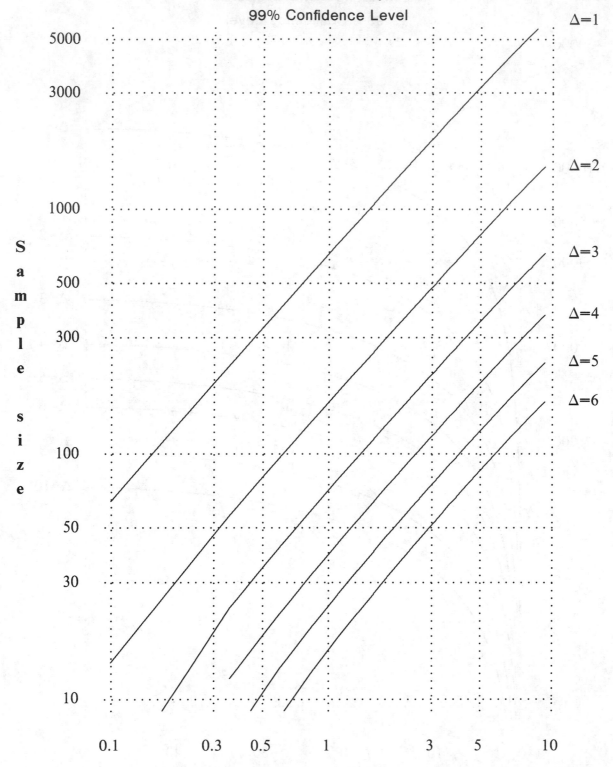

Percent

Figure 5

MINIMUM OBSERVED FAILURES
Failure Rate Estimation

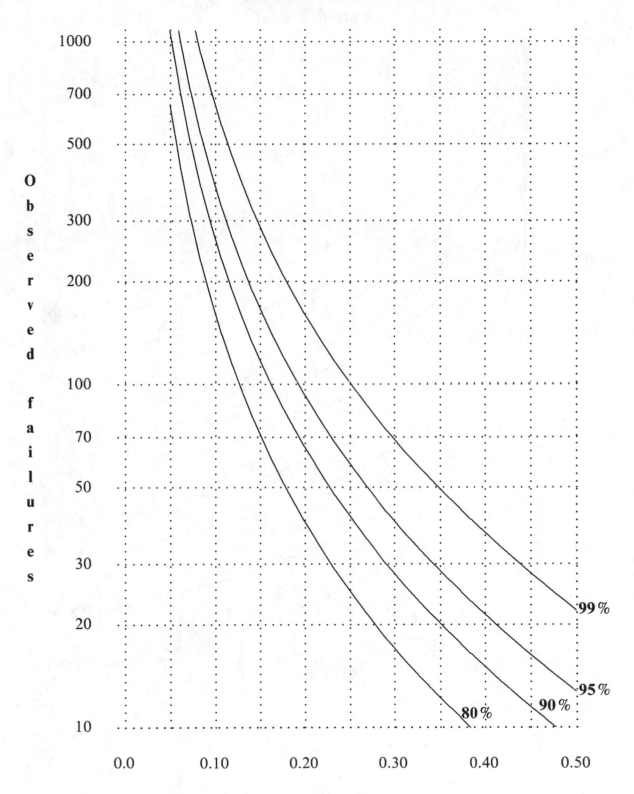

Figure 6

MINIMUM SAMPLE SIZE
Failure Rate Cases
6-Month Interval

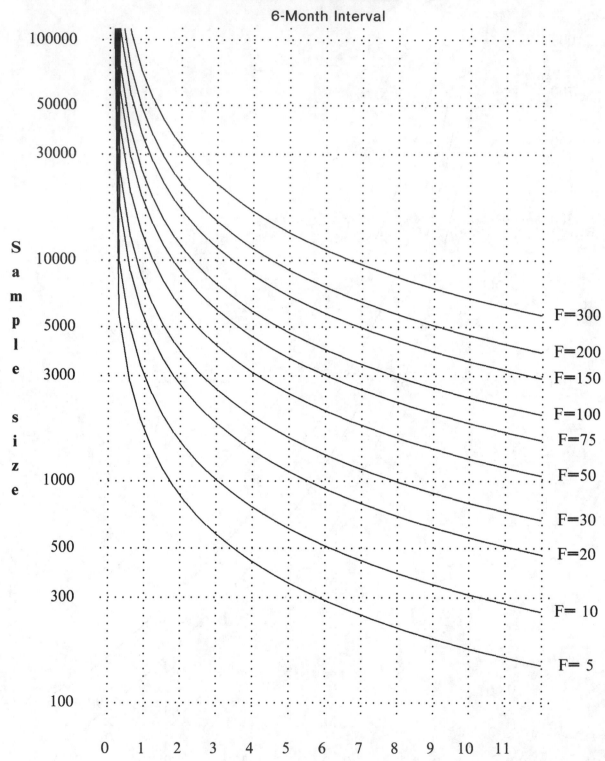

Failure rate: Percent per year

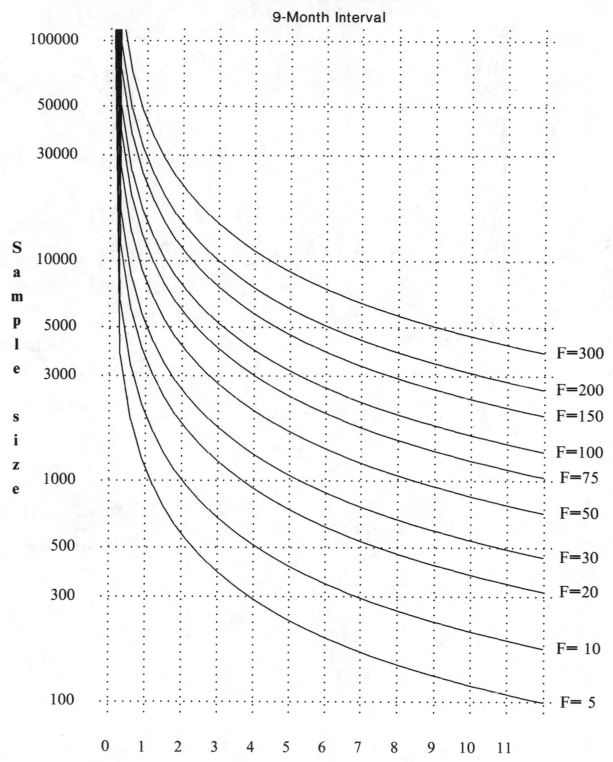

Figure 7

MINIMUM SAMPLE SIZE
Failure Rate Cases
9-Month Interval

F=300
F=200
F=150
F=100
F=75
F=50
F=30
F=20
F= 10
F= 5

Failure rate: Percent per year

47

Figure 8

MINIMUM SAMPLE SIZE
Failure Rate Cases
12-Month Interval

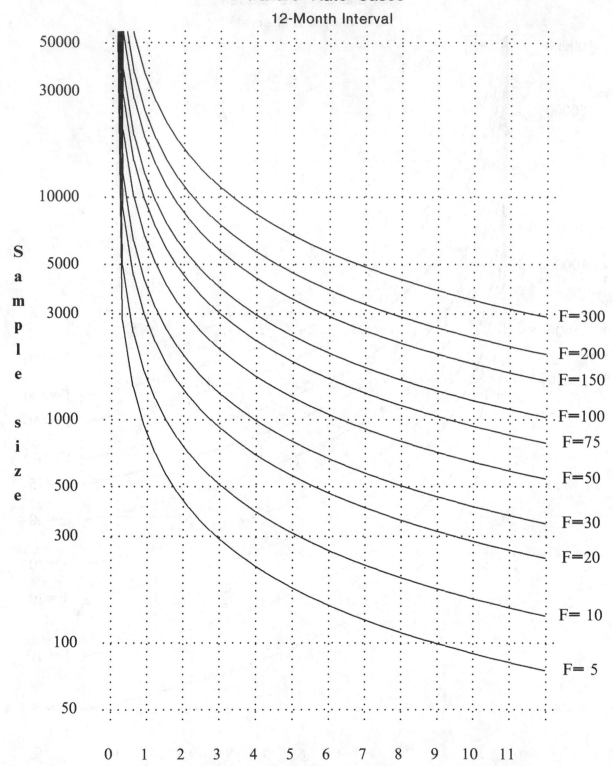

Failure rate: Percent per year

Figure 9

MINIMUM SAMPLE SIZES
Estimating One Normal Mean

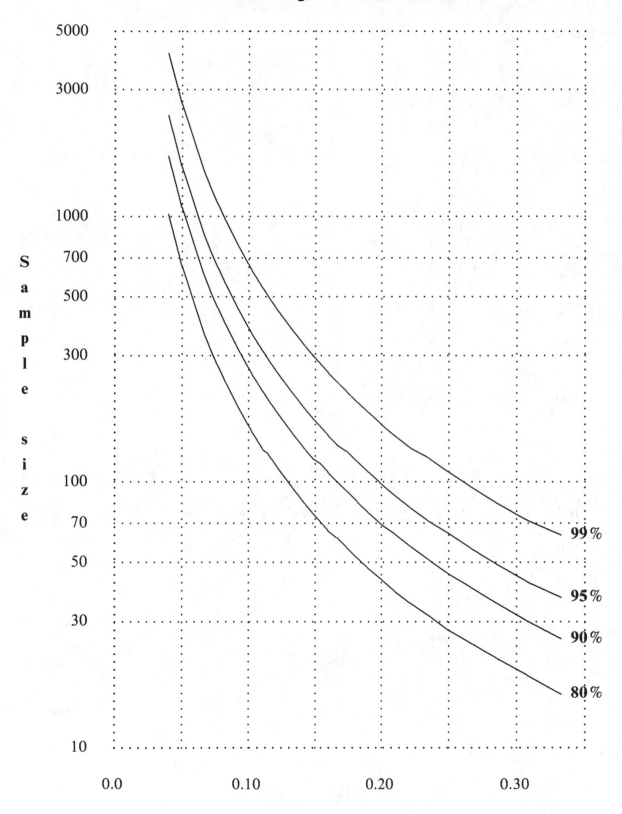

Precision

Figure 10

MINIMUM SAMPLE SIZES
Estimating One Normal Variance

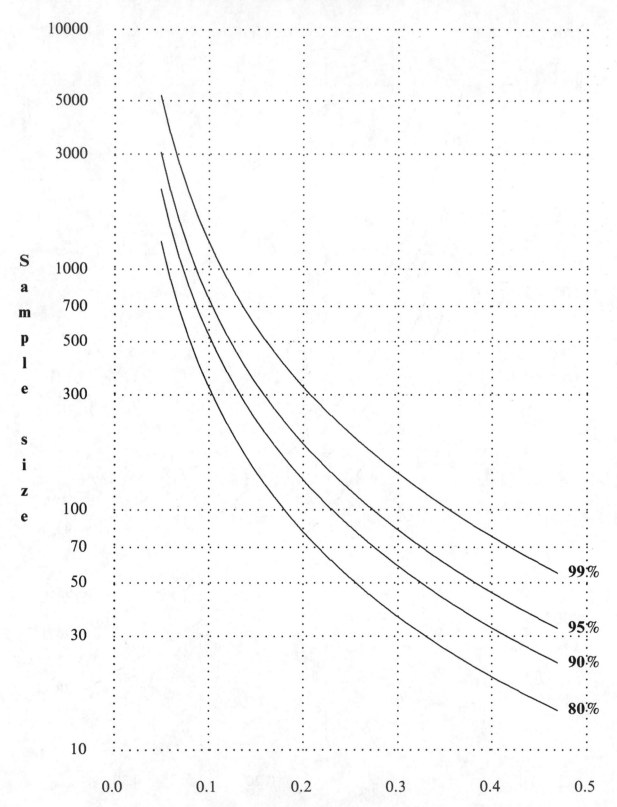

Precision

50

Figure 11

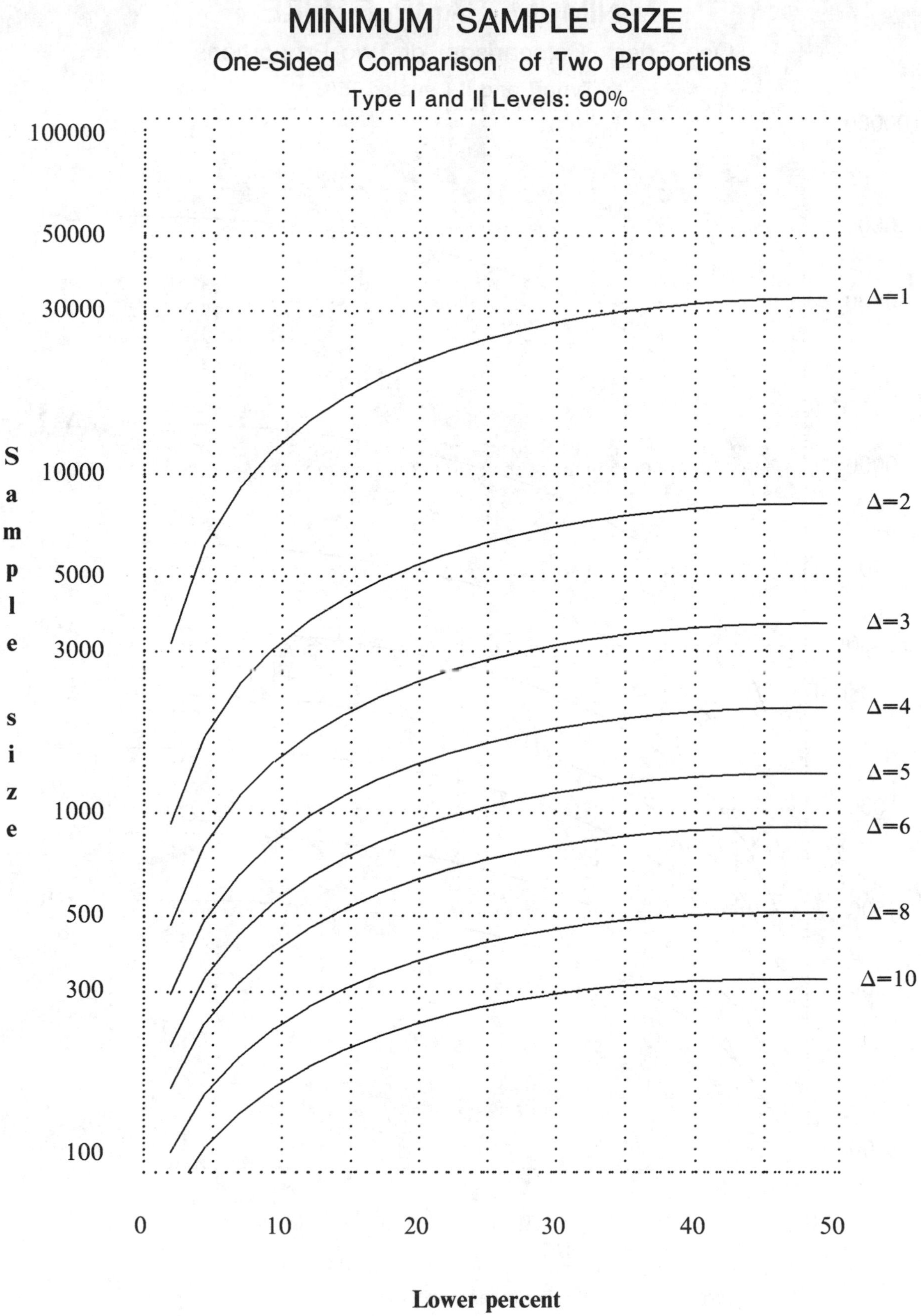

MINIMUM SAMPLE SIZE
One-Sided Comparison of Two Proportions
Type I and II Levels: 90%
100000
50000
30000
10000
5000
3000
1000
500
300
100
Sample size
Δ=1
Δ=2
Δ=3
Δ=4
Δ=5
Δ=6
Δ=8
Δ=10
0
10
20
30
40
50
Lower percent

Figure 12

MINIMUM SAMPLE SIZE
One-Sided Comparison of Two Proportions
Type I and II Levels: 95%

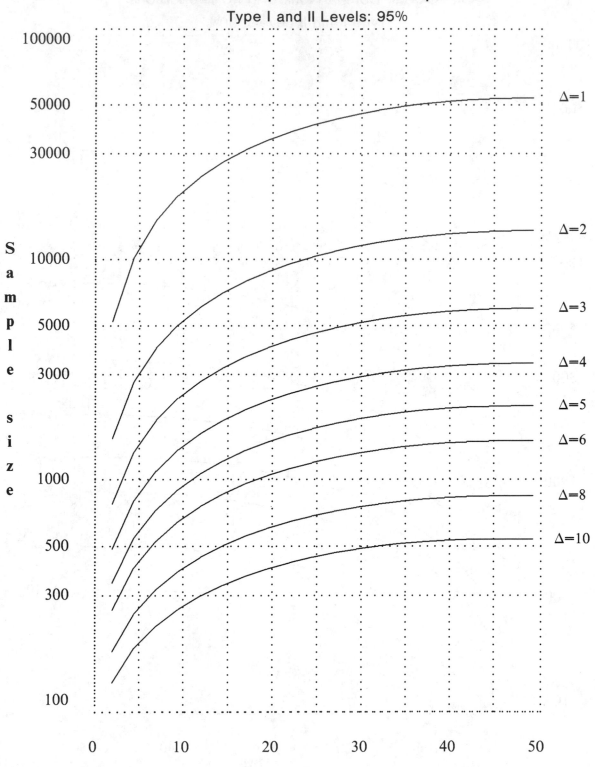

Lower percent

Figure 13

MINIMUM SAMPLE SIZE
One-Sided Comparison of Two Proportions
Type I and II Levels: 99%

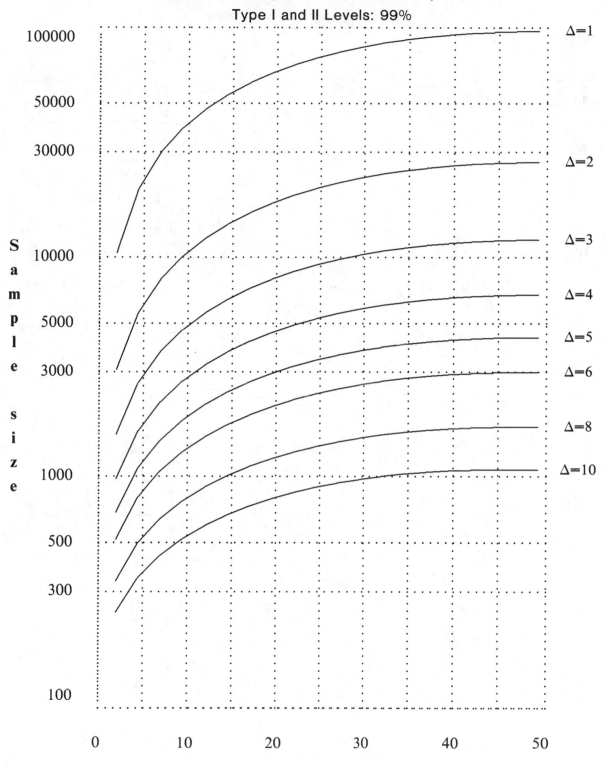

Lower percent

53

Figure 14

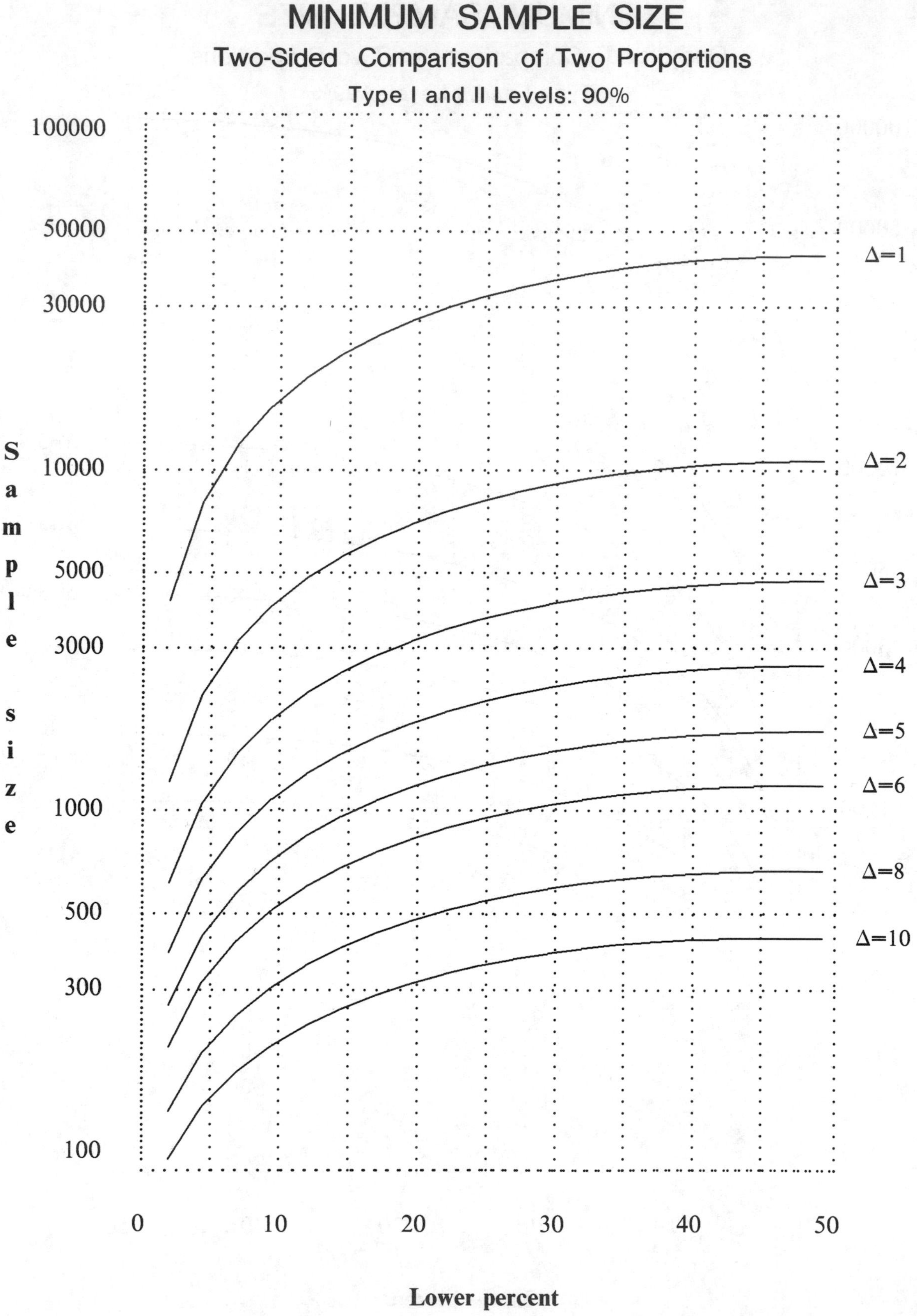
MINIMUM SAMPLE SIZE
Two-Sided Comparison of Two Proportions
Type I and II Levels: 90%
100000
50000
30000
10000
5000
3000
1000
500
300
100
Sample size
Δ=1
Δ=2
Δ=3
Δ=4
Δ=5
Δ=6
Δ=8
Δ=10
0
10
20
30
40
50
Lower percent

Figure 15

MINIMUM SAMPLE SIZE
Two-Sided Comparison of Two Proportions
Type I and II Levels: 95%

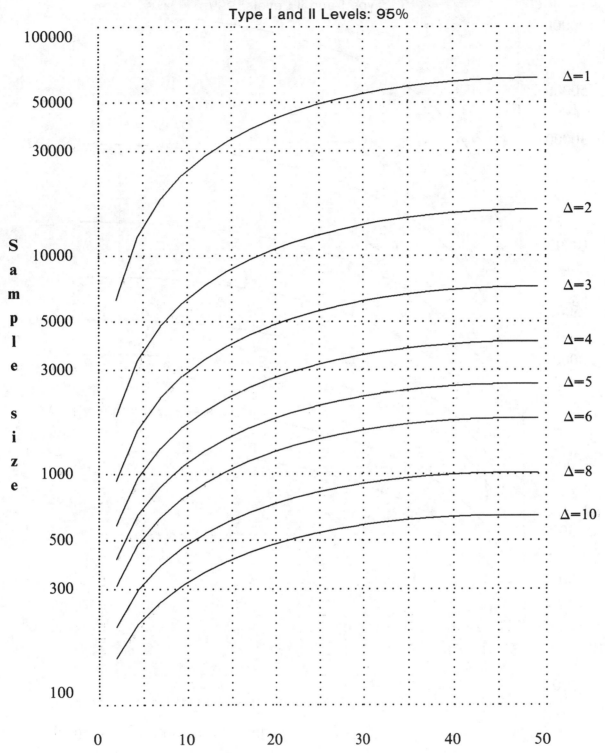

Lower percent

Figure 16

MINIMUM SAMPLE SIZE
Two Sided Comparison of Two Proportions
Type I and II Levels: 99%

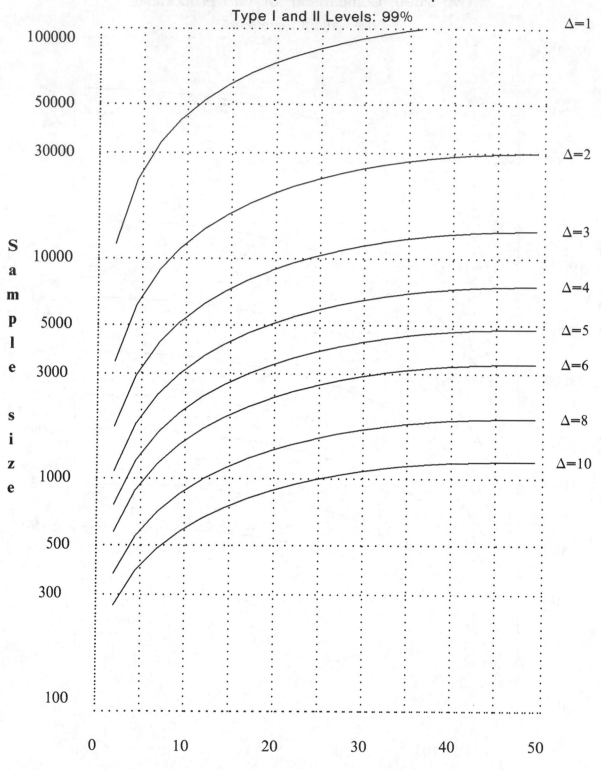

Lower percent

Figure 17

MINIMUM OBSERVED FAILURES
One-Sided Comparison of Two Rates
Type I Level: 90%

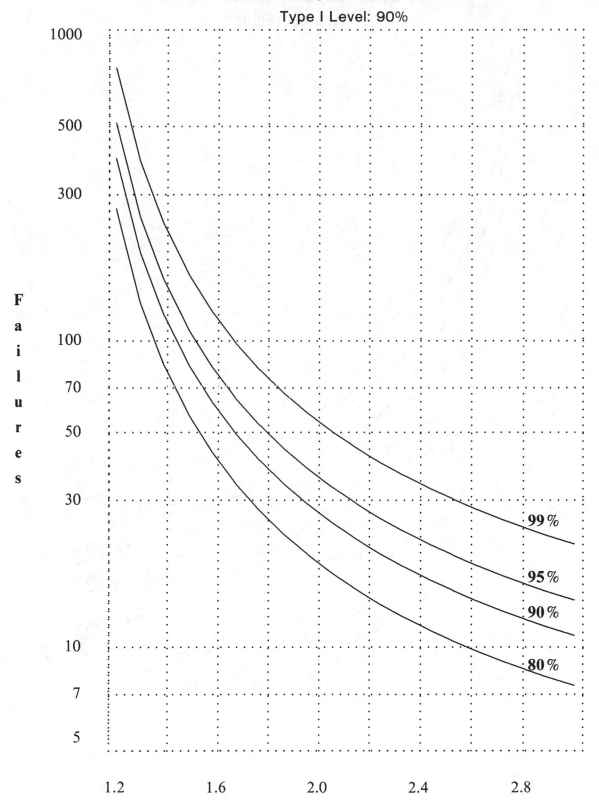

Ratio of rates

Percentages on curves are Type II levels

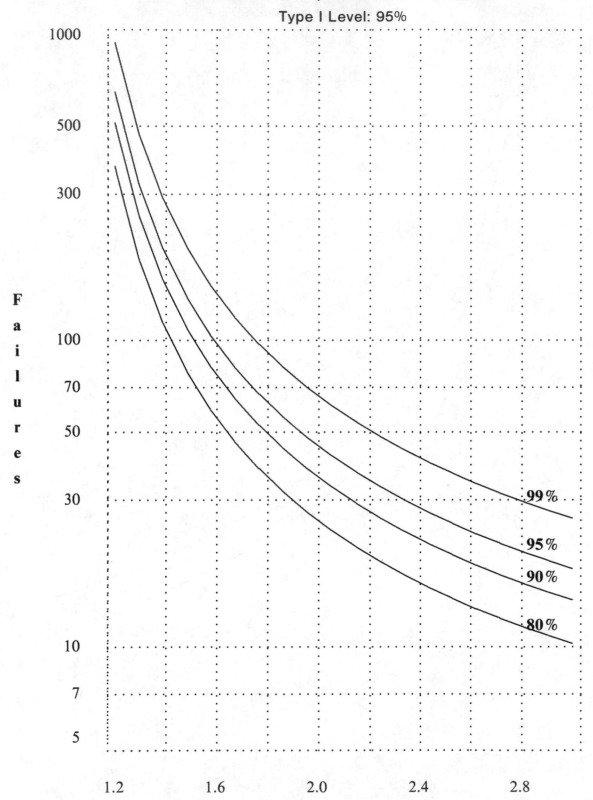

Figure 18

MINIMUM OBSERVED FAILURES

One-Sided Comparison of Two Rates

Type I Level: 95%

Ratio of rates

Percentages on curves are Type II levels

Figure 19

MINIMUM OBSERVED FAILURES
One-Sided Comparison of Two Rates
Type I Level: 99%

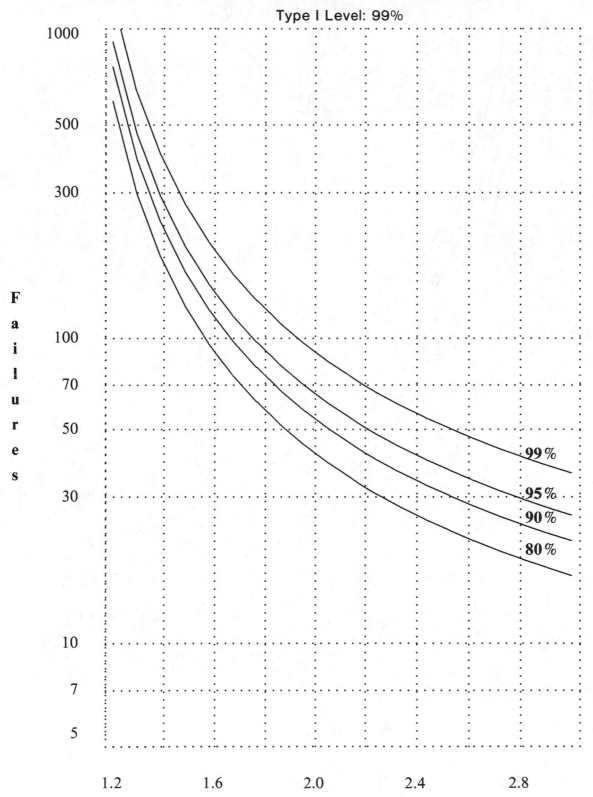

Ratio of rates

Percentages on curves are Type II levels

Figure 20

MINIMUM OBSERVED FAILURES

Two-Sided Comparison of Two Rates

Type I Level: 90%

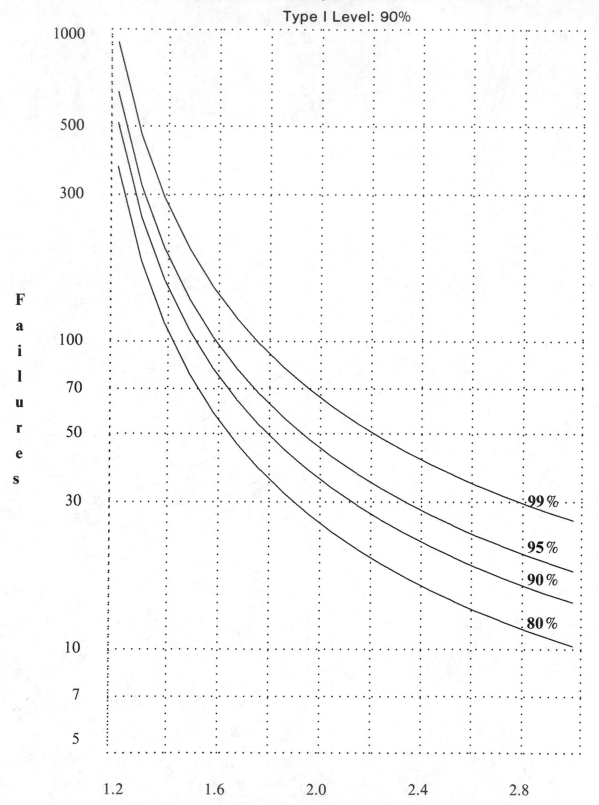

Ratio of rates

Percentages on curves are Type II levels

Figure 21

MINIMUM OBSERVED FAILURES

Two-Sided Comparison of Two Rates

Type I Level: 95%

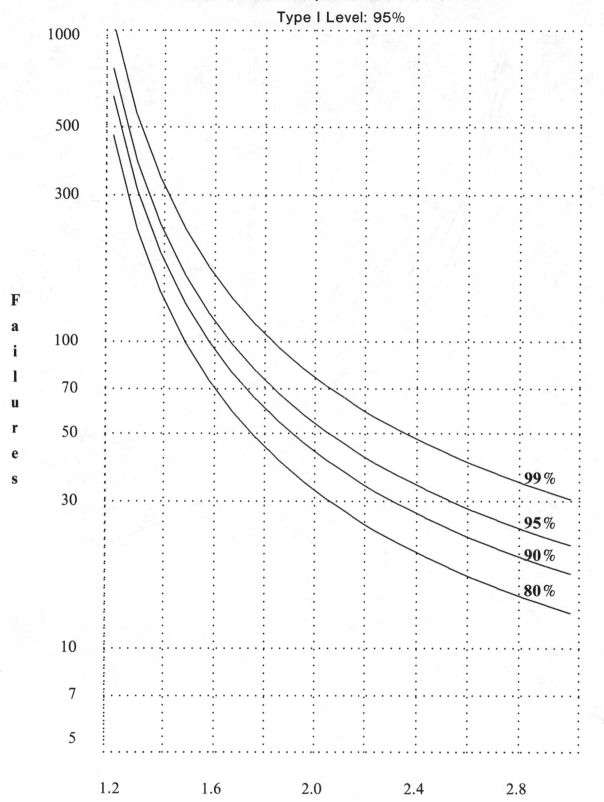

Ratio of rates

Percentages on curves are Type II levels

Figure 22

MINIMUM OBSERVED FAILURES
Two-Sided Comparison of Two Rates
Type I Level: 99%

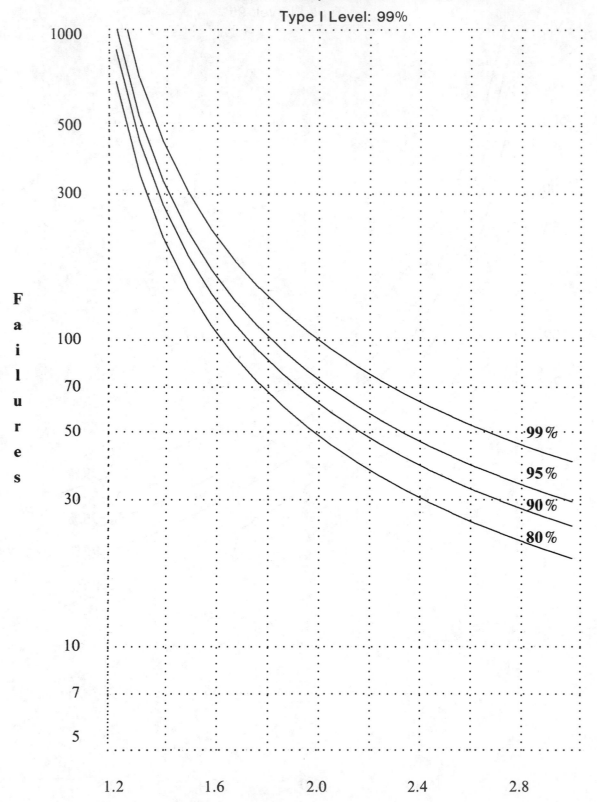

Ratio of rates

Percentages on curves are Type II levels

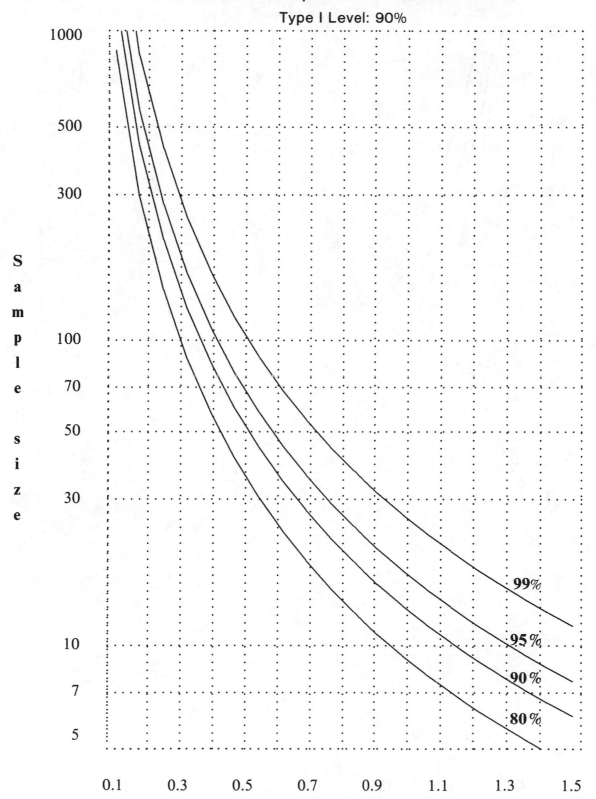

Figure 23

MINIMUM SAMPLE SIZES
One-Sided Comparison of Normal Means
Type I Level: 90%

Ratio of difference in means to standard deviation

Percentages on curves are Type II levels

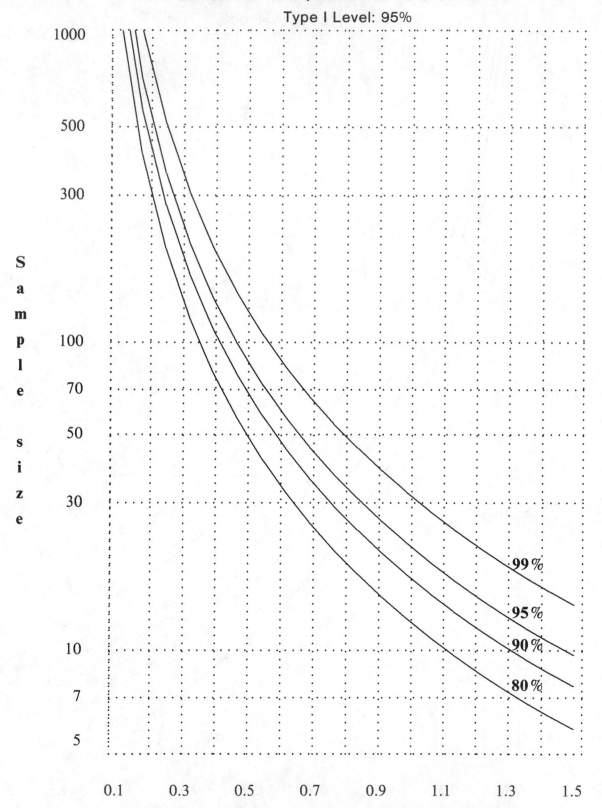

Figure 24

MINIMUM SAMPLE SIZES
One-Sided Comparison of Normal Means
Type I Level: 95%

Sample size

99%

95%

90%

80%

0.1   0.3   0.5   0.7   0.9   1.1   1.3   1.5

Ratio of difference in means to standard deviation

Percentages on curves are Type II levels

64

Figure 25

MINIMUM SAMPLE SIZES
One-Sided Comparison of Normal Means
Type I Level: 99%

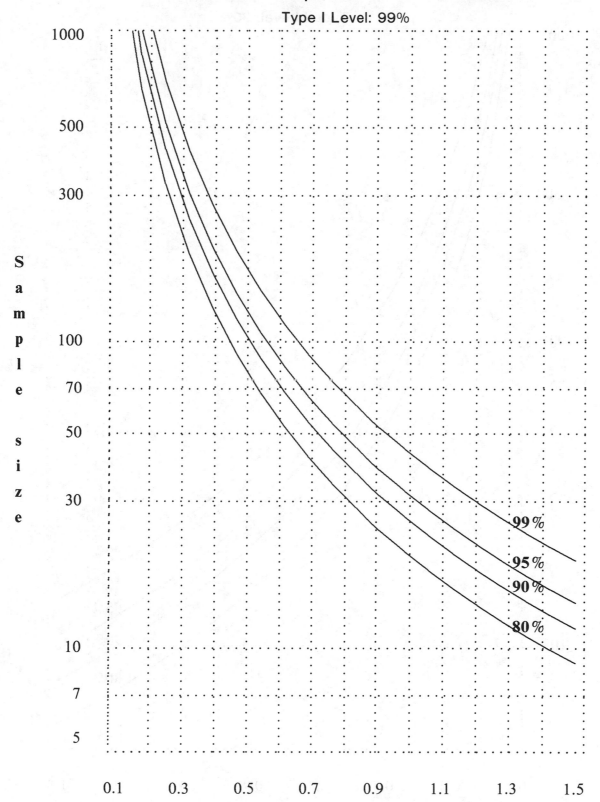

Ratio of difference in means to standard deviation

Percentages on curves are Type II levels

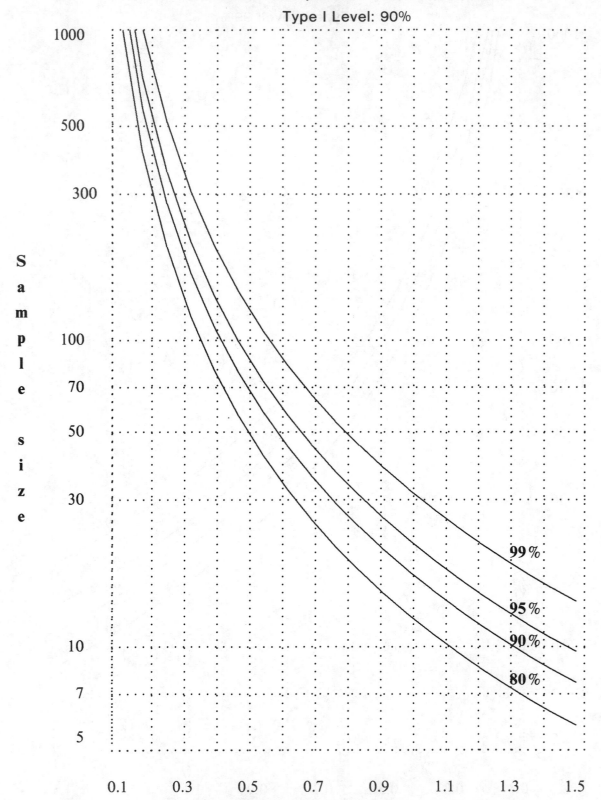

Figure 26

MINIMUM SAMPLE SIZES
Two-Sided Comparison of Normal Means
Type I Level: 90%

Ratio of difference in means to standard deviation

Percentages on curves are Type II levels

Figure 27

MINIMUM SAMPLE SIZES
Two-Sided Comparison of Normal Means
Type I Level: 95%

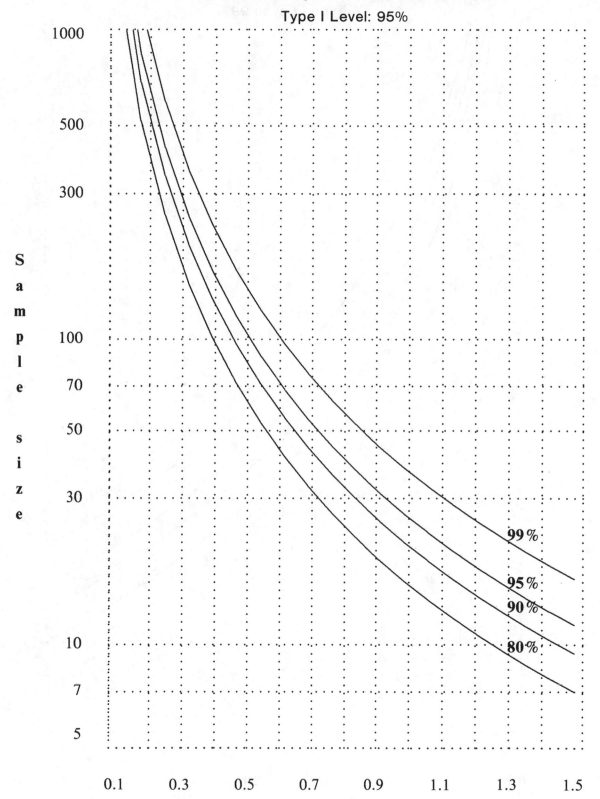

Ratio of differences in means to standard deviation

Percentages on curves are Type II levels

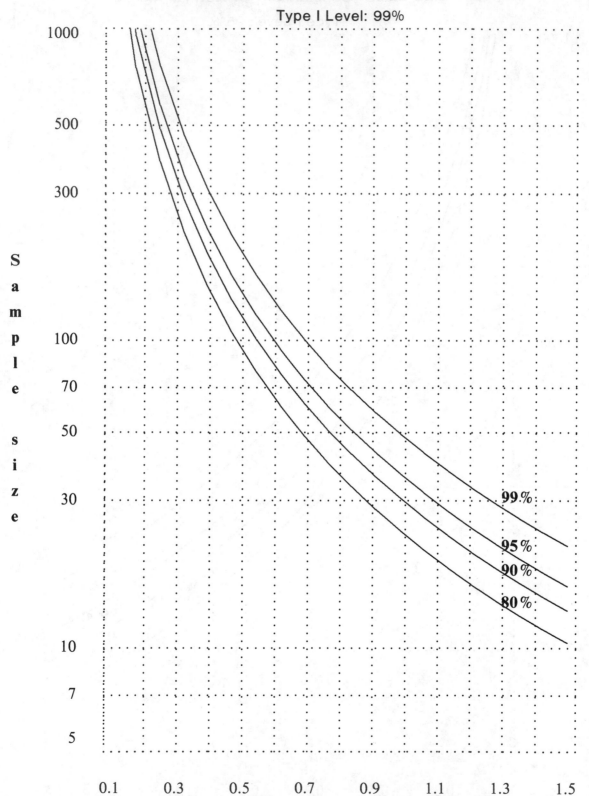

Figure 28

MINIMUM SAMPLE SIZES
Two-Sided Comparison of Normal Means
Type I Level: 99%

Ratio of differences in means to standard deviation

Percentages on curves are Type II levels

Figure 29

MINIMUM SAMPLE SIZES
Comparing Two Variances
Type I Level: 90%

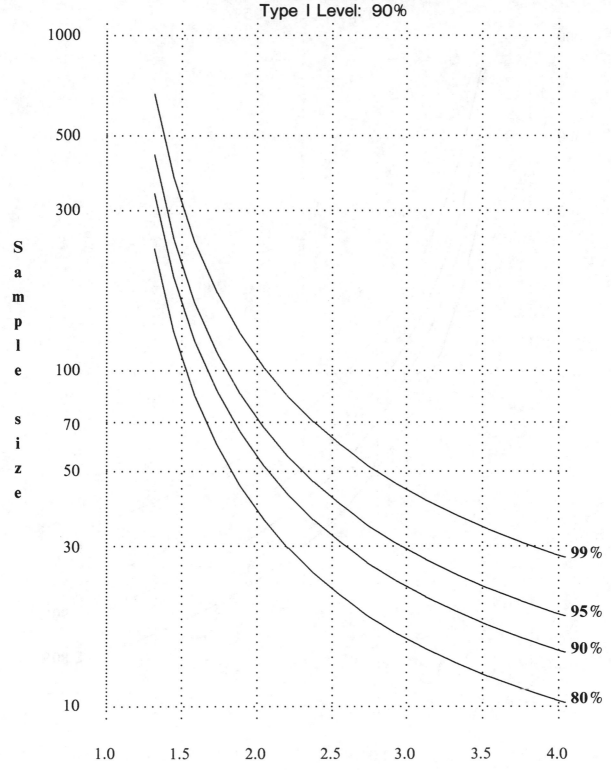

Ratio of variances

Percentages on curves are Type II levels

Figure 30

MINIMUM SAMPLE SIZES
Comparing Two Variances
Type I Level: 95%

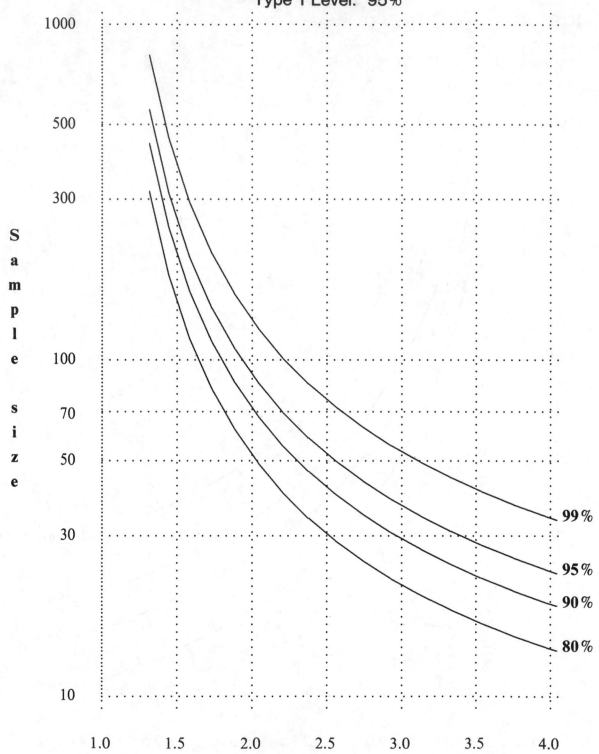

Ratio of variances

Percentages on curves are Type II levels

Figure 31

MINIMUM SAMPLE SIZES
Comparing Two Variances
Type I Level: 99%

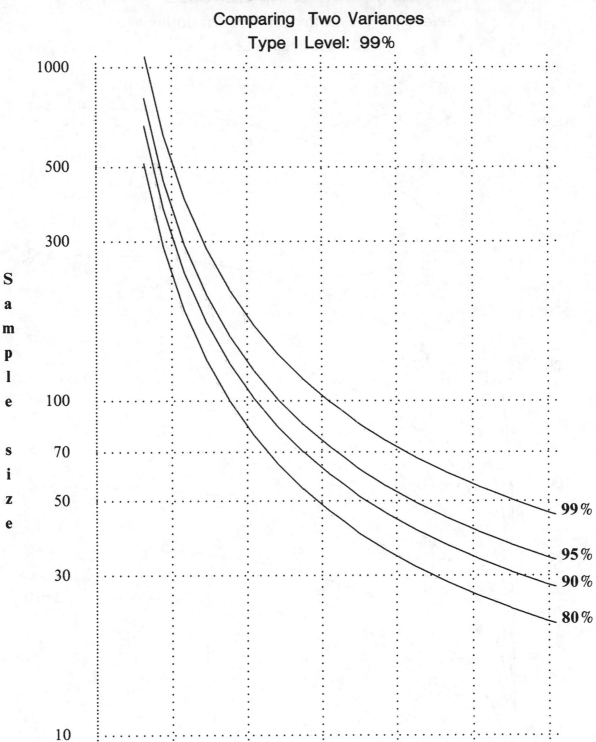

Ratio of variances

Percentages on curves are Type II levels

71

Figure 32

MINIMUM SAMPLE SIZE
Selecting the Better of Two Proportions
80% Confidence Level

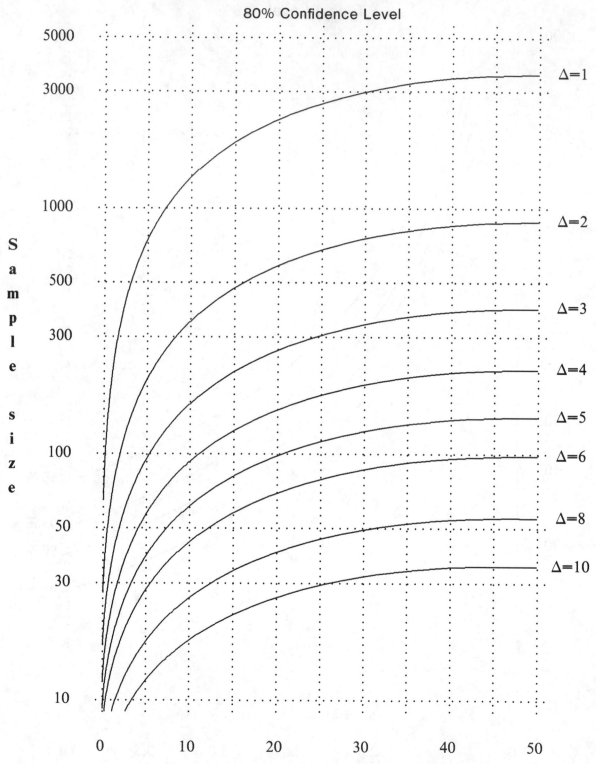

Percent

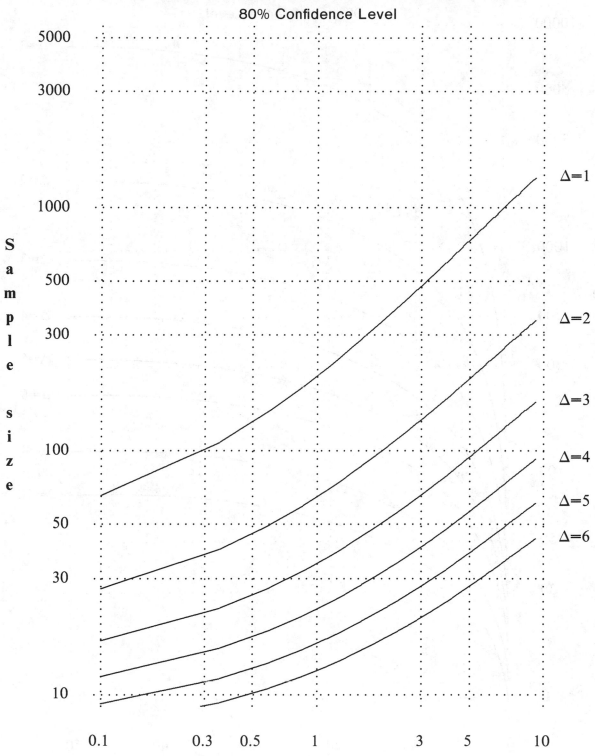

Figure 32A

MINIMUM SAMPLE SIZE
Selecting the Better of Two Proportions
80% Confidence Level

Figure 33

MINIMUM SAMPLE SIZE
Selecting the Better of Two Proportions
90% Confidence Level

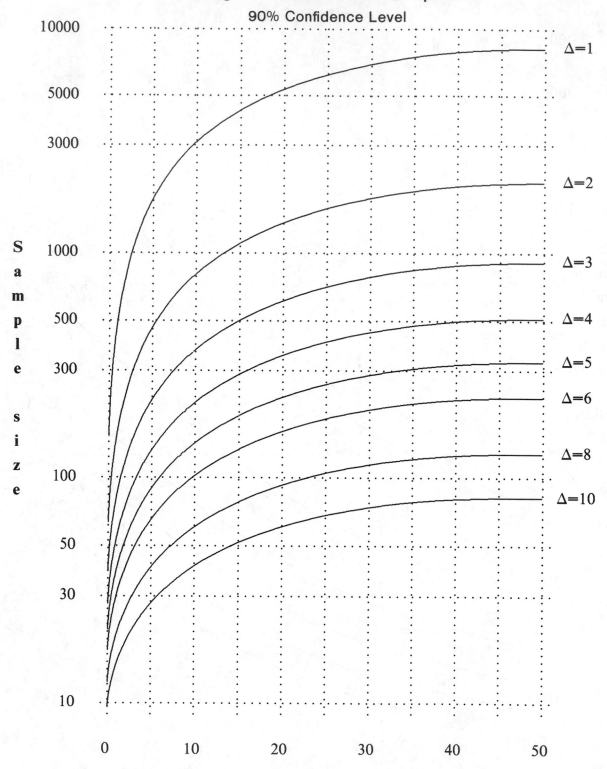

Percent

MINIMUM SAMPLE SIZE
Selecting the Better of Two Proportions
90% Confidence Level

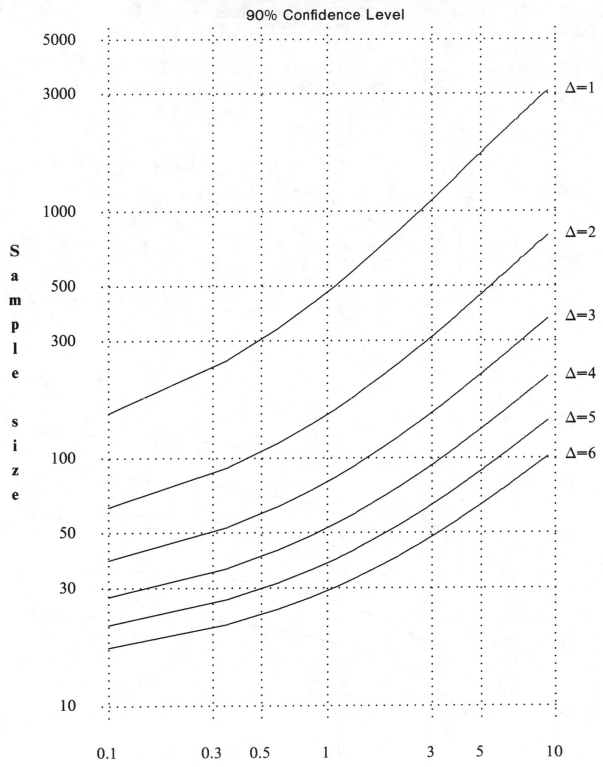

Percent

Figure 34

MINIMUM SAMPLE SIZE
Selecting the Better of Two Proportions
95% Confidence Level

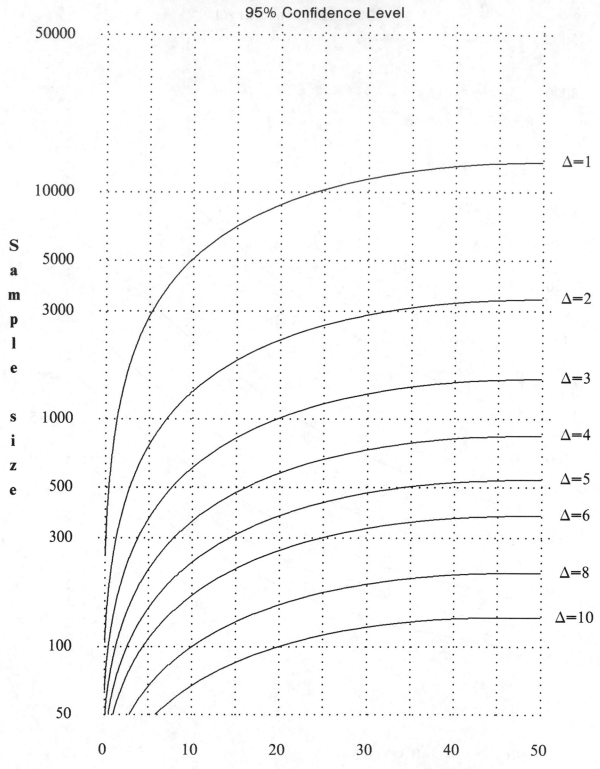

Percent

MINIMUM SAMPLE SIZE
Selecting the Better of Two Proportions
95% Confidence Level

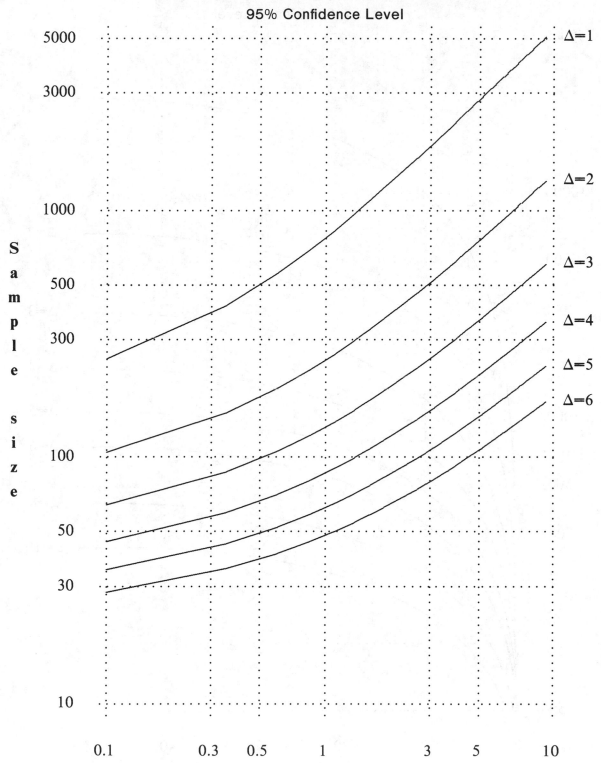

Percent

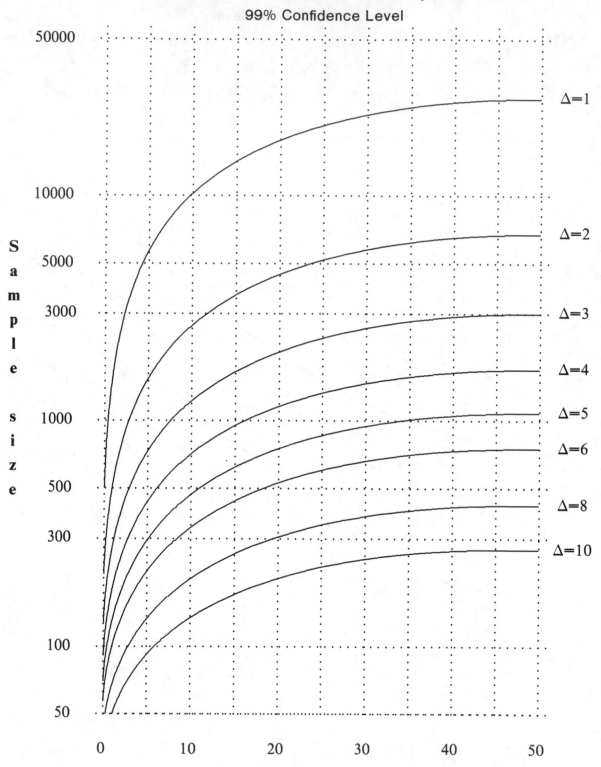

Figure 35

MINIMUM SAMPLE SIZE
Selecting the Better of Two Proportions
99% Confidence Level

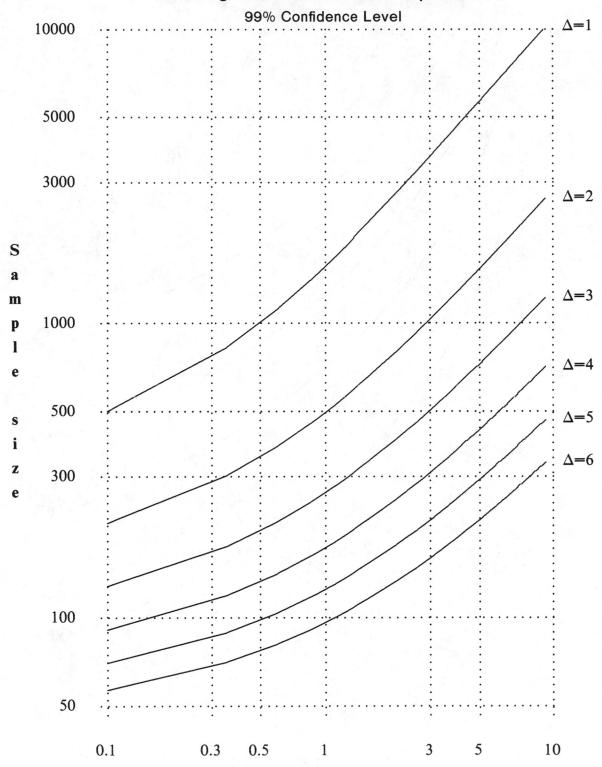

Figure 35A

MINIMUM SAMPLE SIZE
Selecting the Better of Two Proportions
99% Confidence Level

Sample size

Percent

Figure 36

MINIMUM OBSERVED FAILURES
Selecting the Better of Two Rates

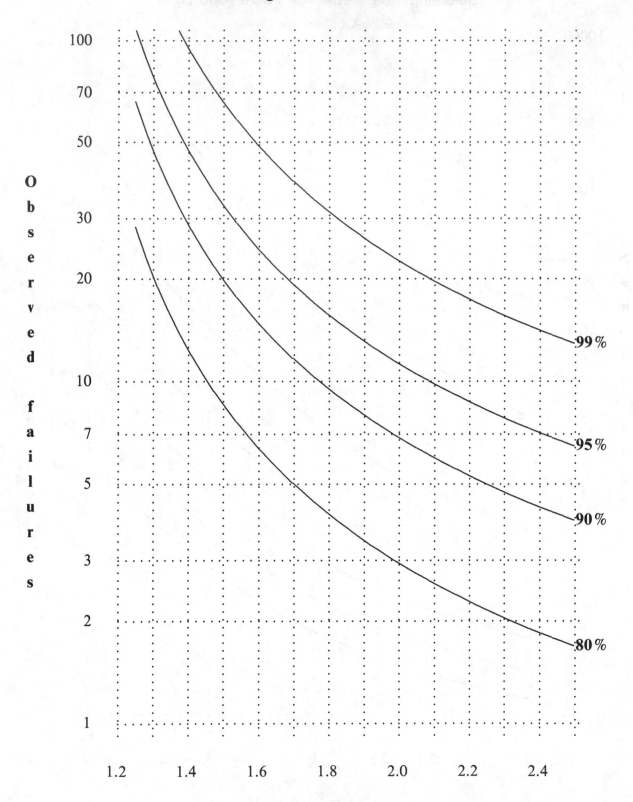

Ratio of rates

Figure 37

MINIMUM SAMPLE SIZES
Selecting the Better of Two Normal Means

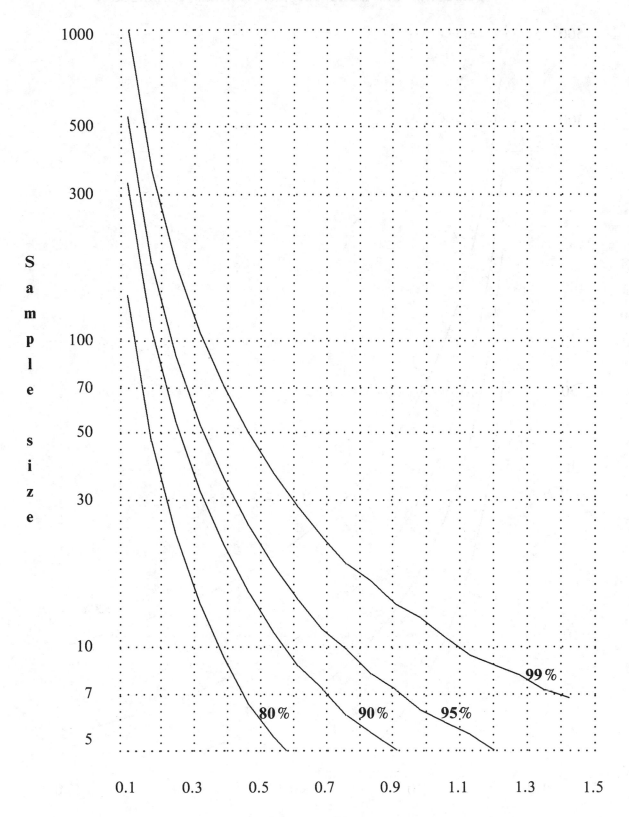

Ratio of difference in means to standard deviation

Figure 38

MINIMUM SAMPLE SIZES
Selecting the Better of Two Normal Variances

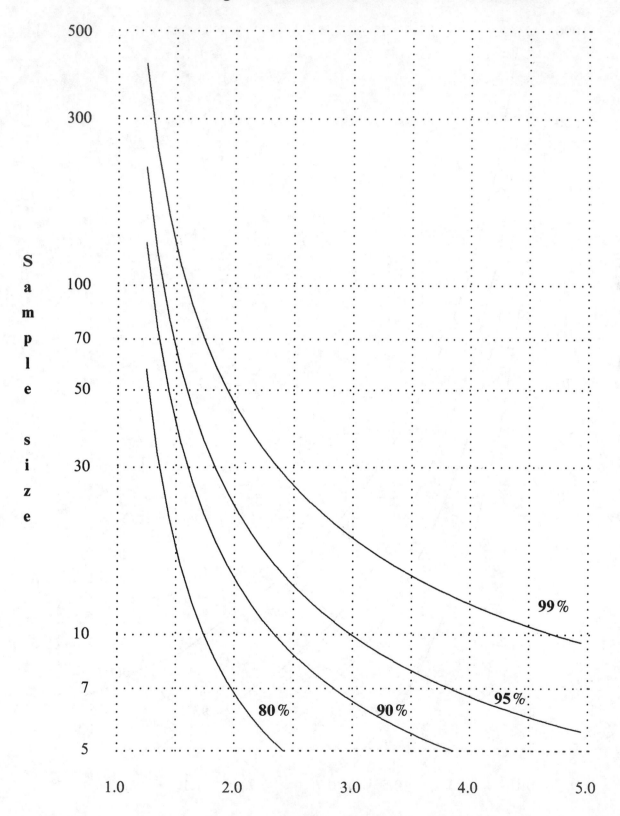

Sample size

Ratio of variances

Figure 39

MINIMUM SAMPLE SIZE
Hypothesis Test: One Proportion
$\Phi_0 = 1\%$

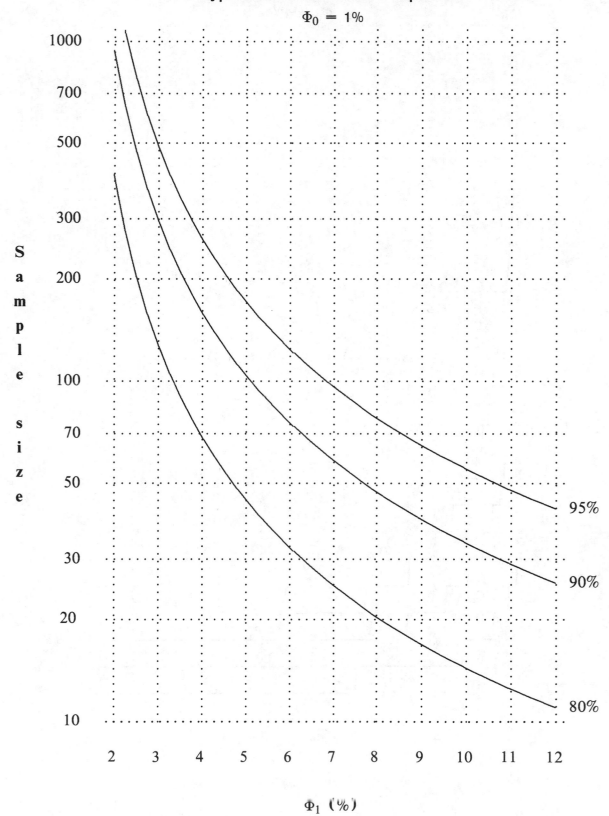

$\Phi_1 \; (\%)$

Figure 40

ACCEPTANCE NUMBERS
Hypothesis Test: One Proportion
$\Phi_0 = 1\%$

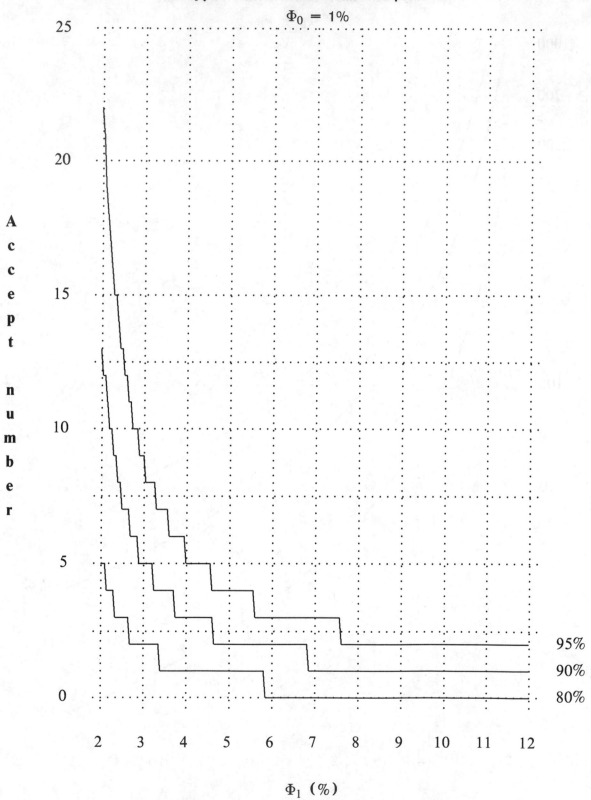

Figure 41

MINIMUM SAMPLE SIZE
Hypothesis Test: One Proportion
$\Phi_0 = 2\%$

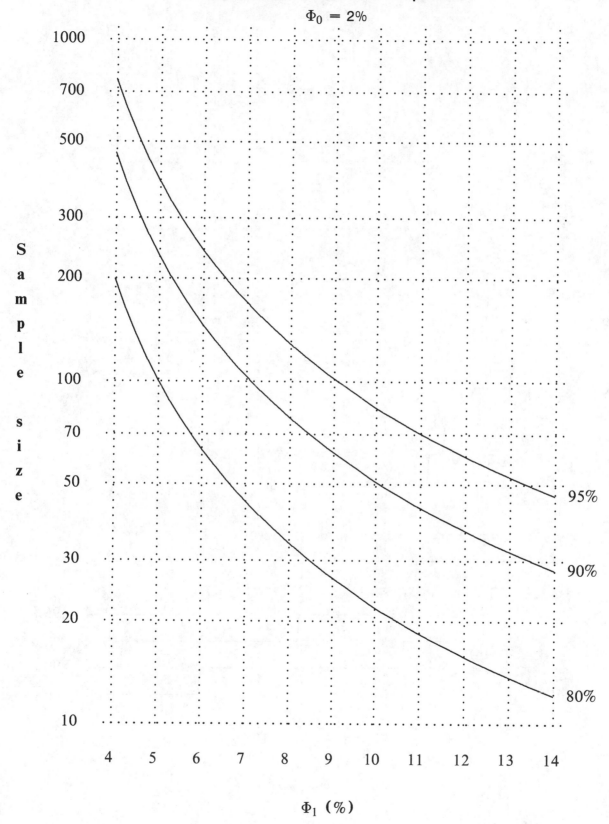

Φ_1 (%)

Figure 42

ACCEPTANCE NUMBERS
Hypothesis Test: One Proportion
$\Phi_0 = 2\%$

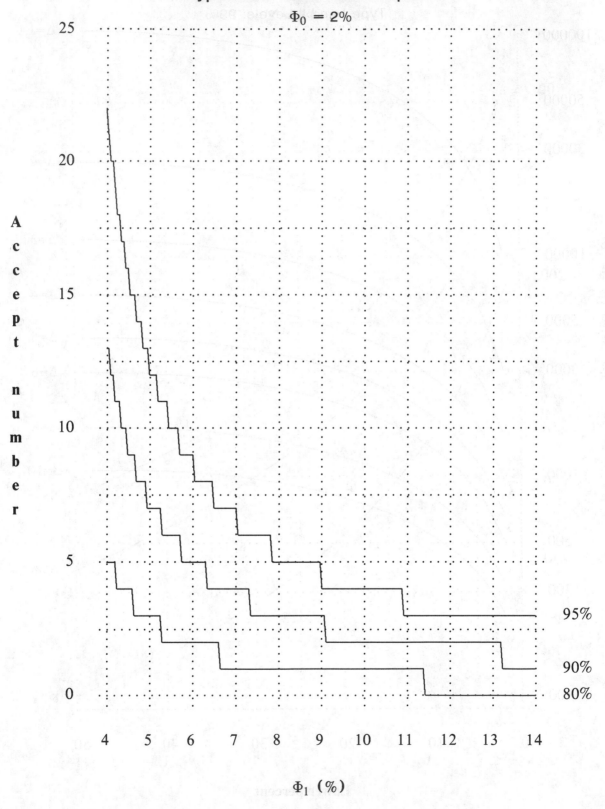

Φ_1 (%)

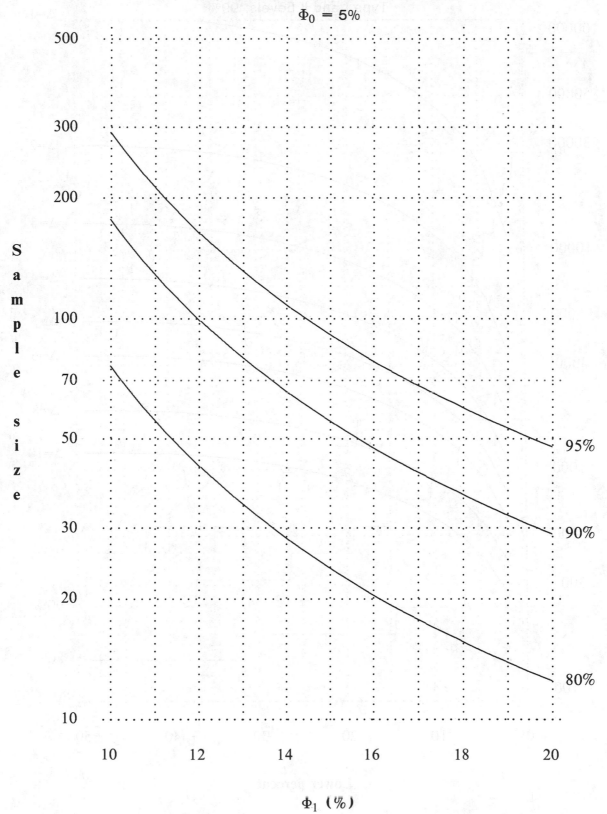

Figure 43

MINIMUM SAMPLE SIZE
Hypothesis Test: One Proportion
$\Phi_0 = 5\%$

$\Phi_1 \ (\%)$

Figure 44

ACCEPTANCE NUMBERS
Hypothesis Test: One Proportion
$\Phi_0 = 5\%$

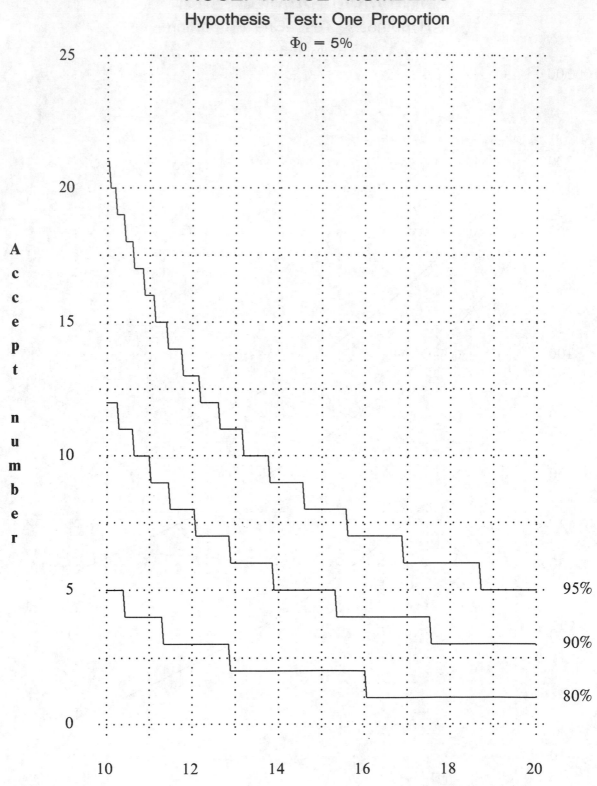

$\Phi_1\ (\%)$

Figure 45

MINIMUM SAMPLE SIZE
Hypothesis Test: One Proportion
$\Phi_0 = 10\%$

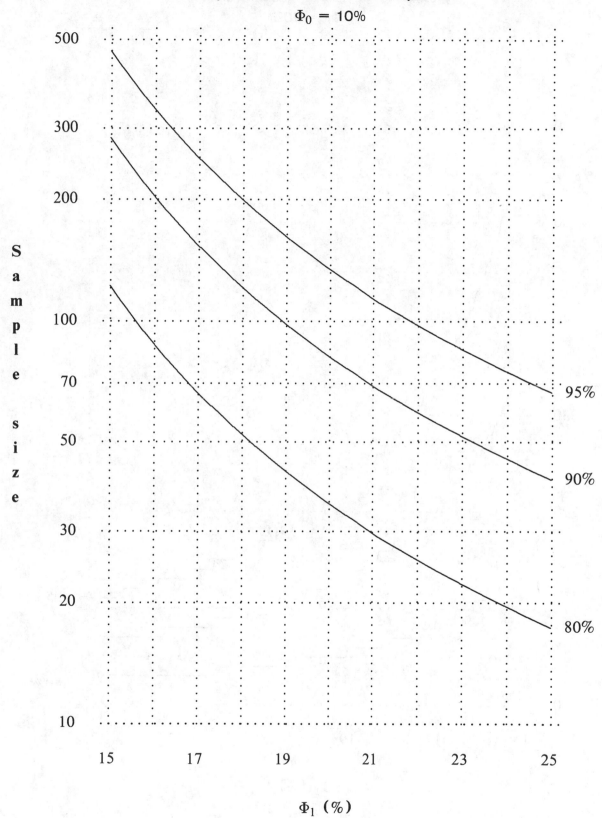

Φ_1 (%)

Figure 46

ACCEPTANCE NUMBERS
Hypothesis Test: One Proportion
$$\Phi_0 = 10\%$$

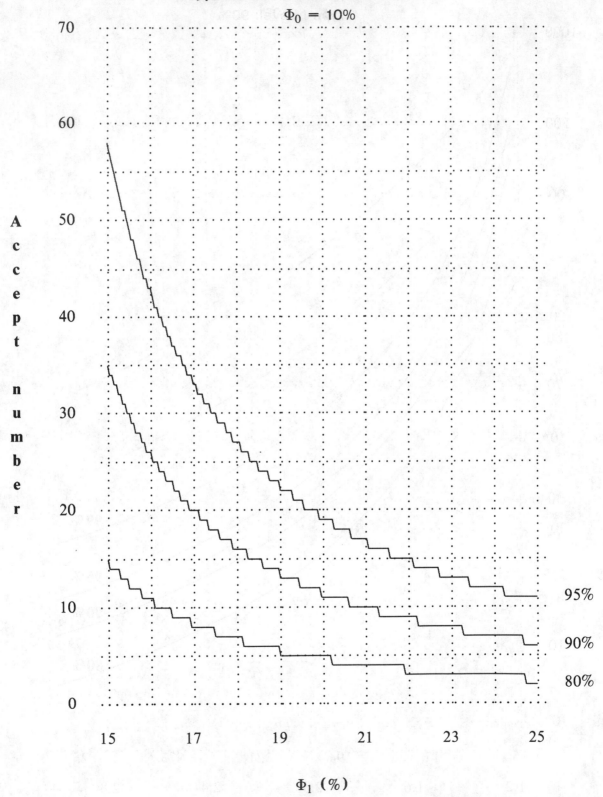

Φ_1 (%)

Figure 47

MINIMUM OBSERVED FAILURES

Hypothesis Test: One Rate
Type I Level: 90%

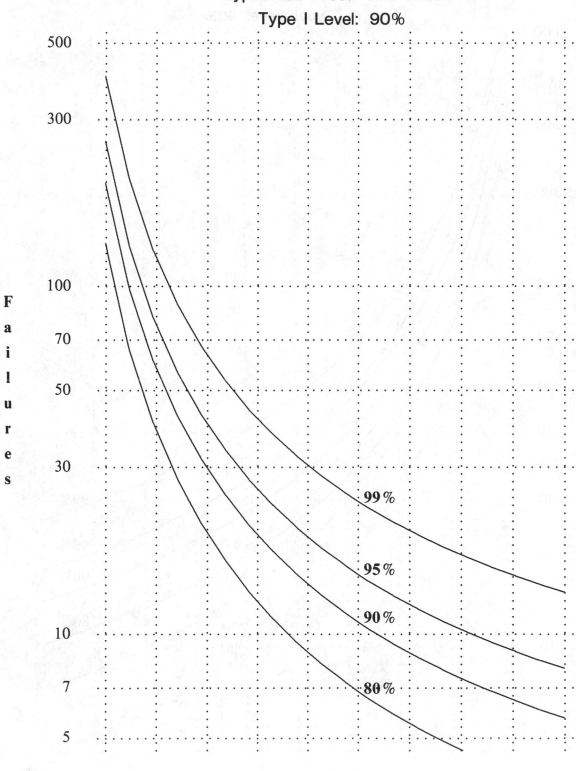

Ratio of hypothesized rates

Percentages on curves are Type II levels

Figure 48

MINIMUM OBSERVED FAILURES

Hypothesis Test: One Rate

Type I Level: 95%

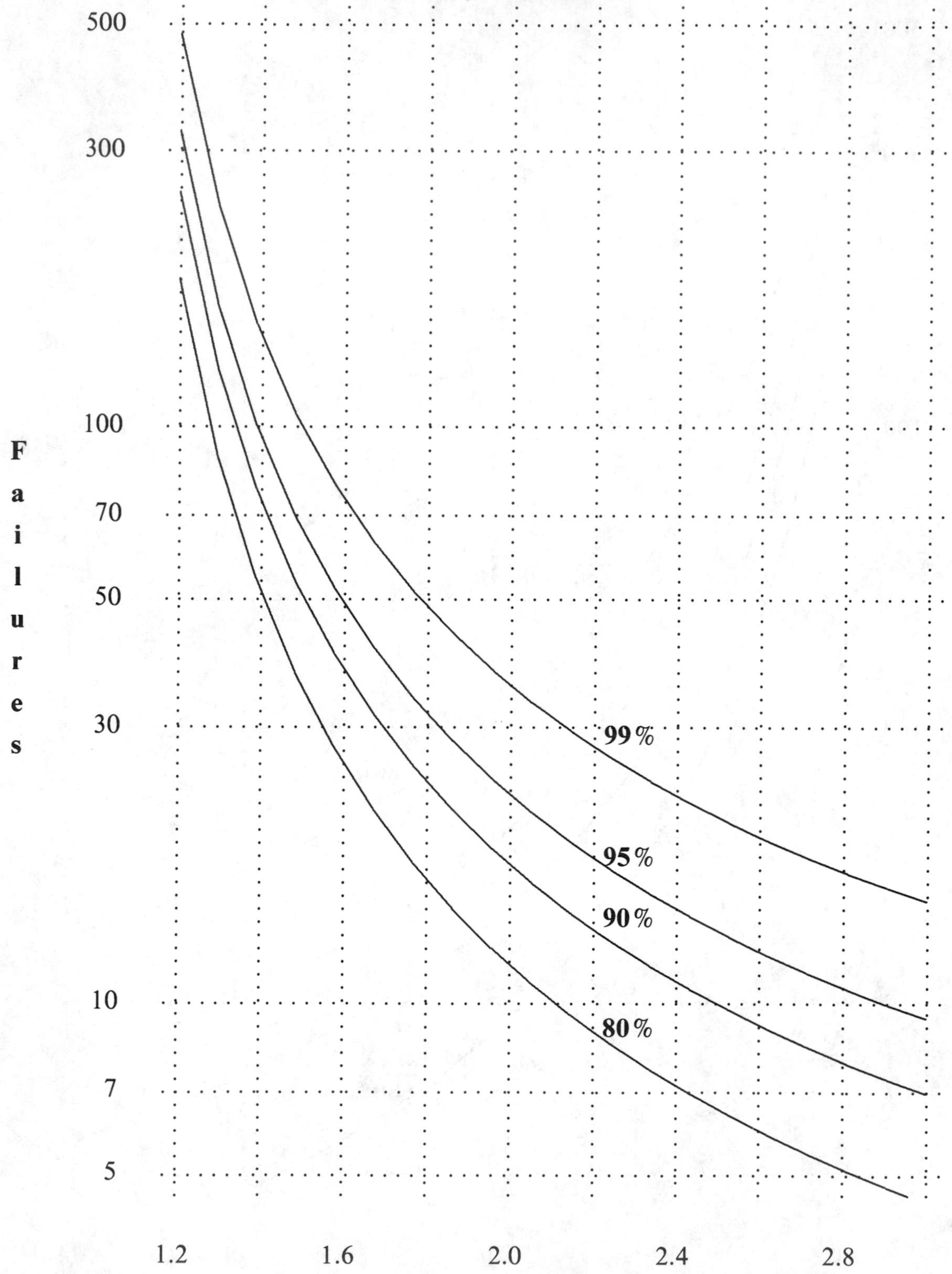

Ratio of hypothesized rates

Percentages on curves are Type II levels

Figure 49

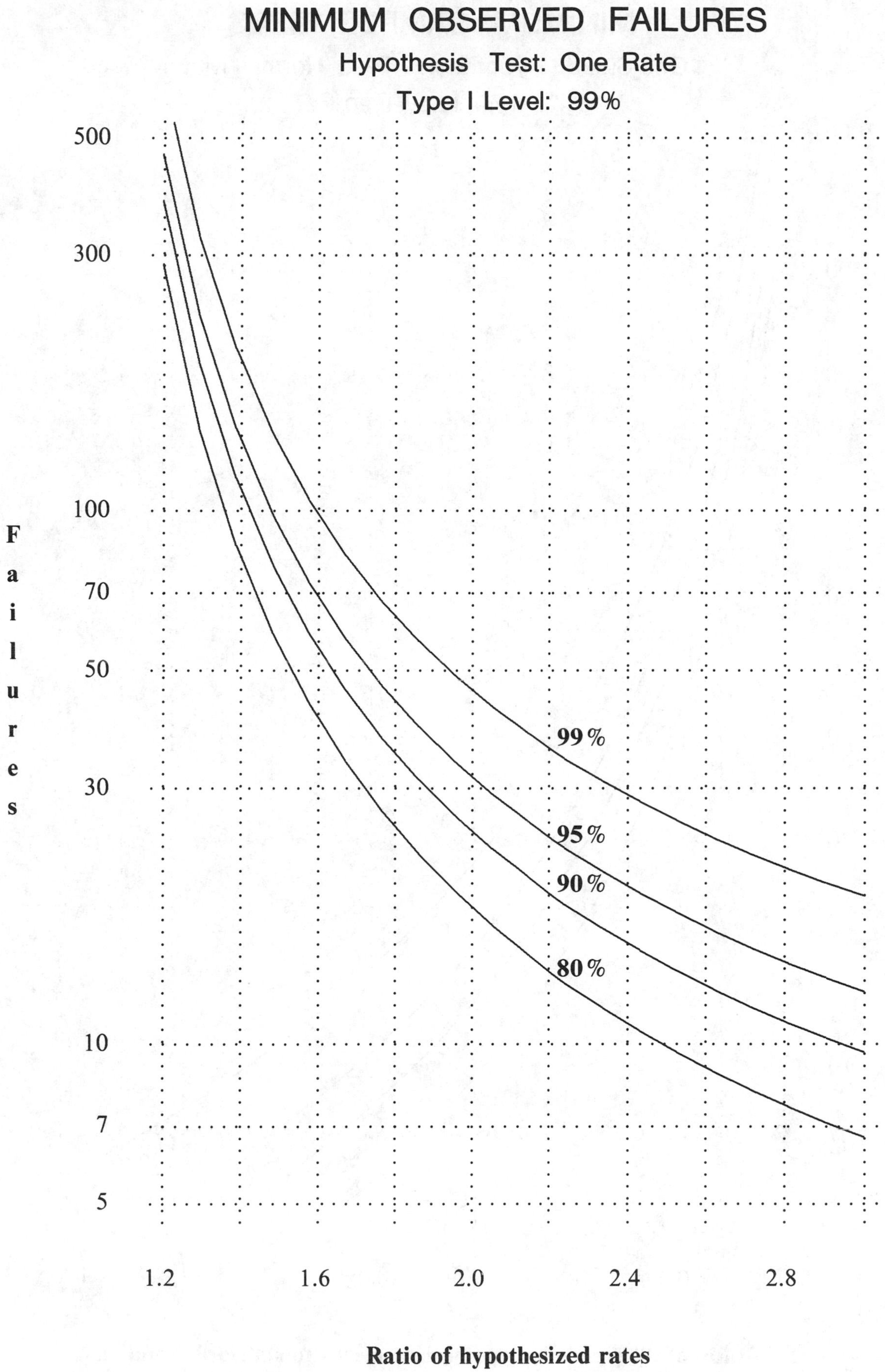

MINIMUM OBSERVED FAILURES
Hypothesis Test: One Rate
Type I Level: 99%
500
300
100
70
50
30
10
7
5
Failures
99%
95%
90%
80%
1.2
1.6
2.0
2.4
2.8
Ratio of hypothesized rates

Percentages on curves are Type II levels

Figure 50

MINIMUM SAMPLE SIZES
One-Sided Hypothesis Test: Normal Mean
Type I Level: 90%

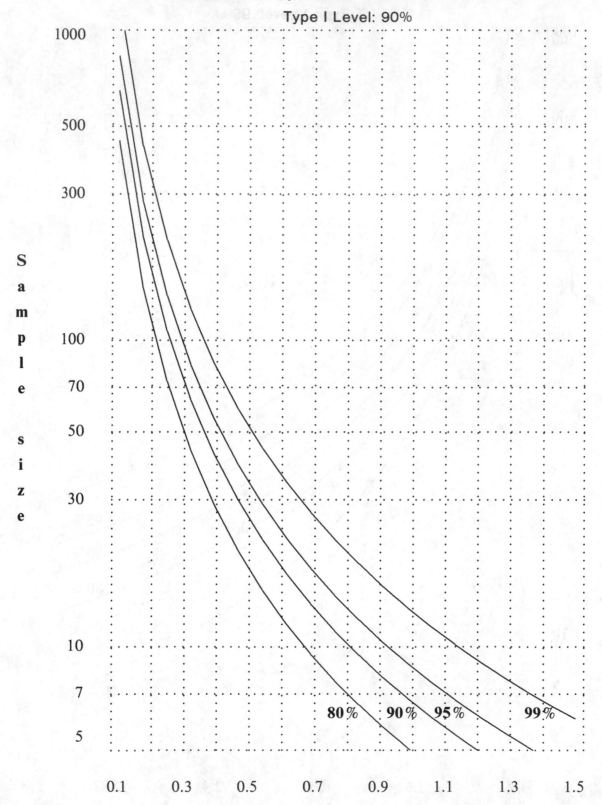

Ratio of difference in hypothesized means to standard deviation

Percentages on curves are Type II levels

Figure 51

MINIMUM SAMPLE SIZES
One-Sided Hypothesis Test: Normal Mean
Type I Level: 95%

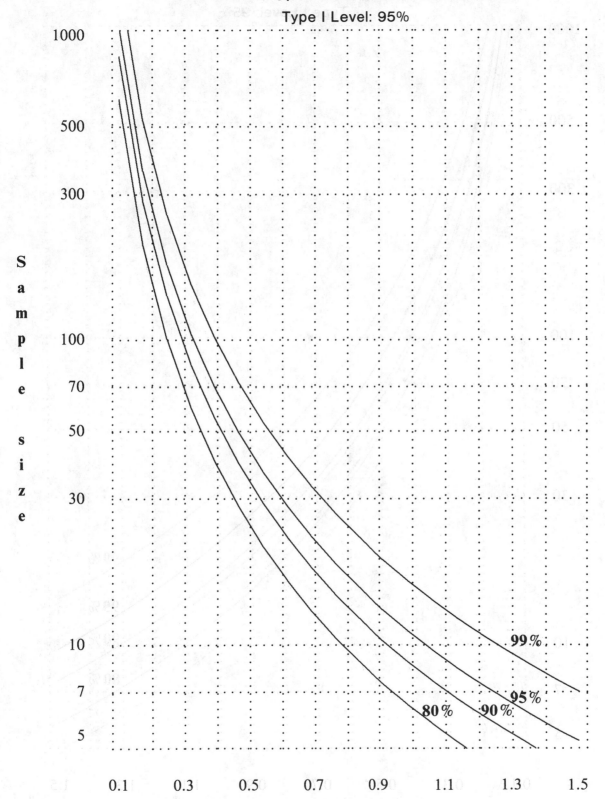

Ratio of difference in hypothesized means to standard deviation

Percentages on curves are Type II levels

Figure 52

MINIMUM SAMPLE SIZES

One-Sided Hypothesis Test: Normal Mean

Type I Level: 99%

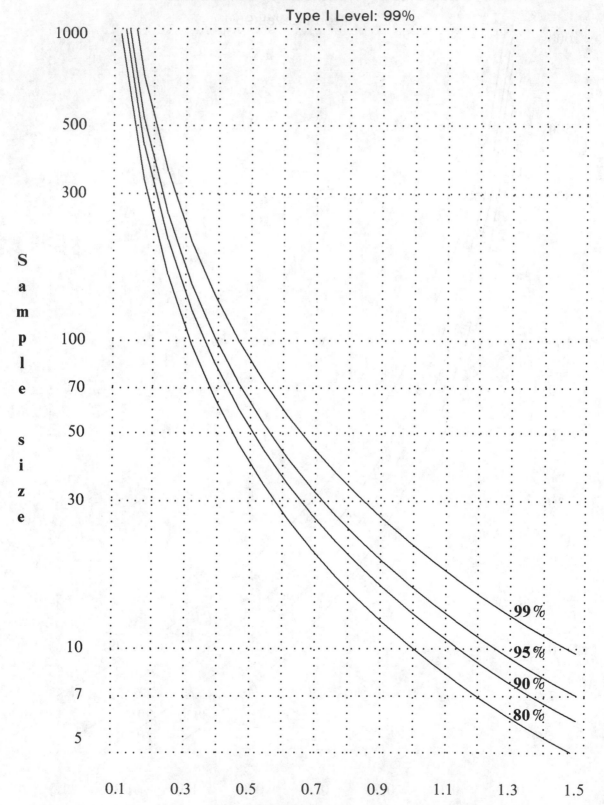

Ratio of difference in hypothesized means to standard deviation

Percentages on curves are Type II levels

Figure 53

MINIMUM SAMPLE SIZES
Two-Sided Hypothesis Test: Normal Mean
Type I Level: 90%

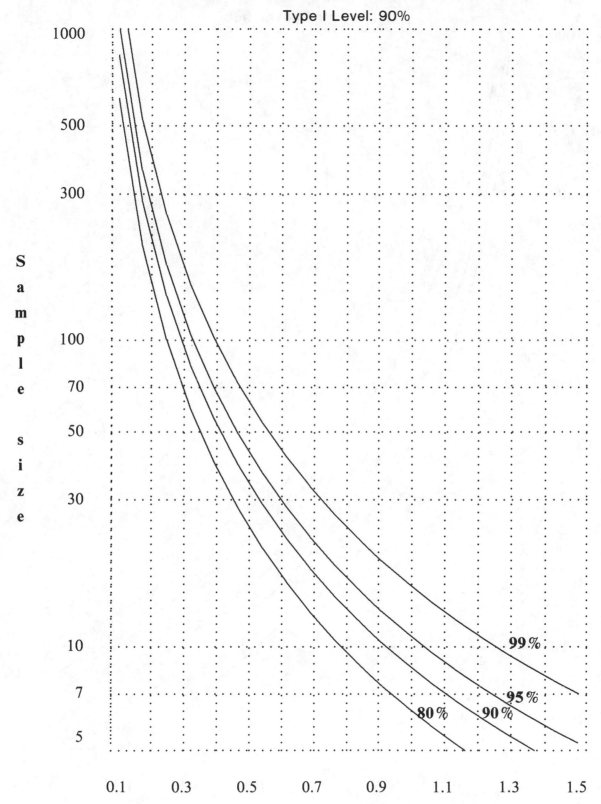

Ratio of difference in hypothesized means to standard deviation

Percentages on curves are Type II levels

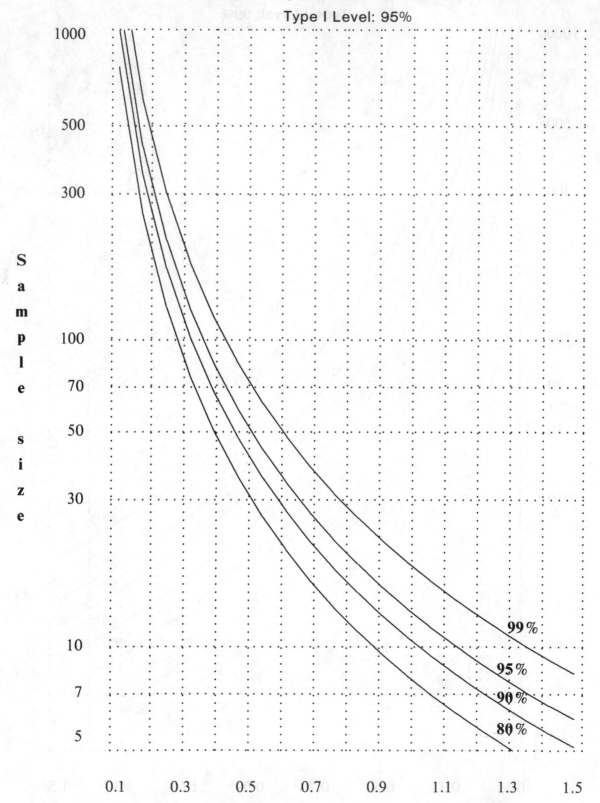

Figure 54

MINIMUM SAMPLE SIZES
Two-Sided Hypothesis Test: Normal Mean
Type I Level: 95%

Ratio of difference in hypothesized means to standard deviation

Percentages on curves are Type II levels

Figure 55
MINIMUM SAMPLE SIZES
Two-Sided Hypothesis Test: Normal Mean
Type I Level: 99%

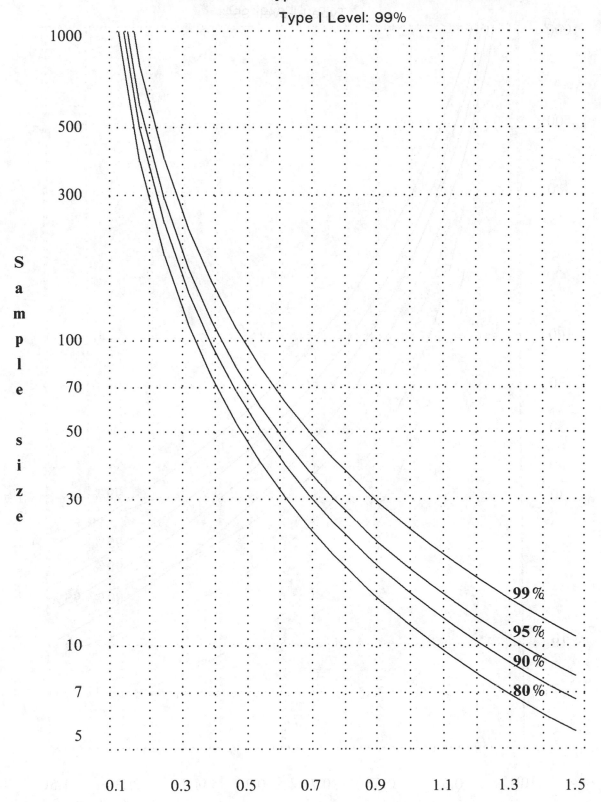

Ratio of difference in hypothesized means to standard deviation

Percentages on curves are Type II levels

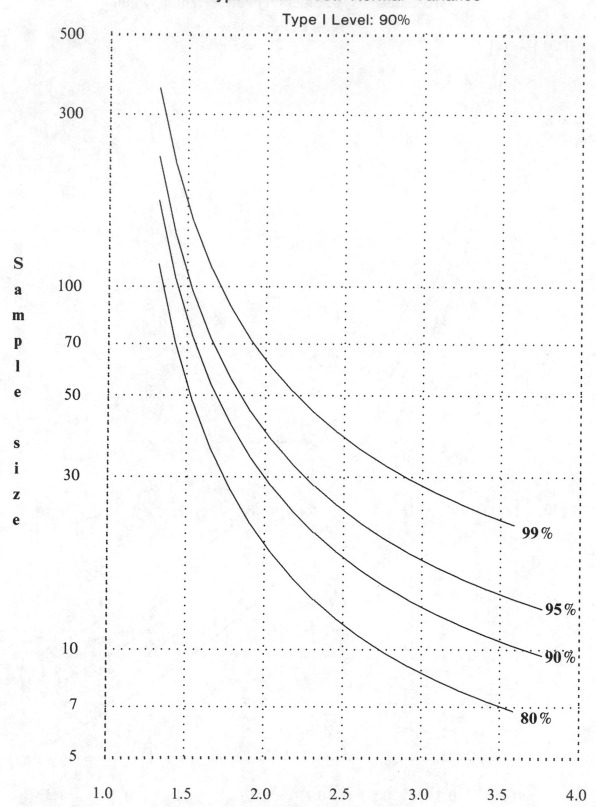

Figure 56

MINIMUM SAMPLE SIZES
Hypothesis Test: Normal Variance
Type I Level: 90%

Ratio of hypothesized variances

Percentages on curves are Type II levels

Figure 57

MINIMUM SAMPLE SIZES
Hypothesis Test: Normal Variance
Type I Level: 95%

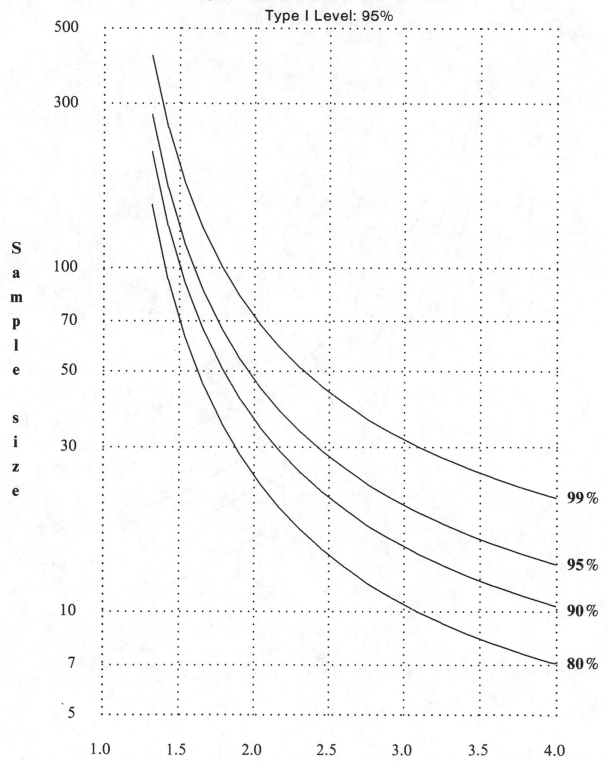

Ratio of hypothesized variances

Percentages on curves are Type II levels

Figure 58

MINIMUM SAMPLE SIZES
Hypothesis Test: Normal Variance
Type I Level: 99%

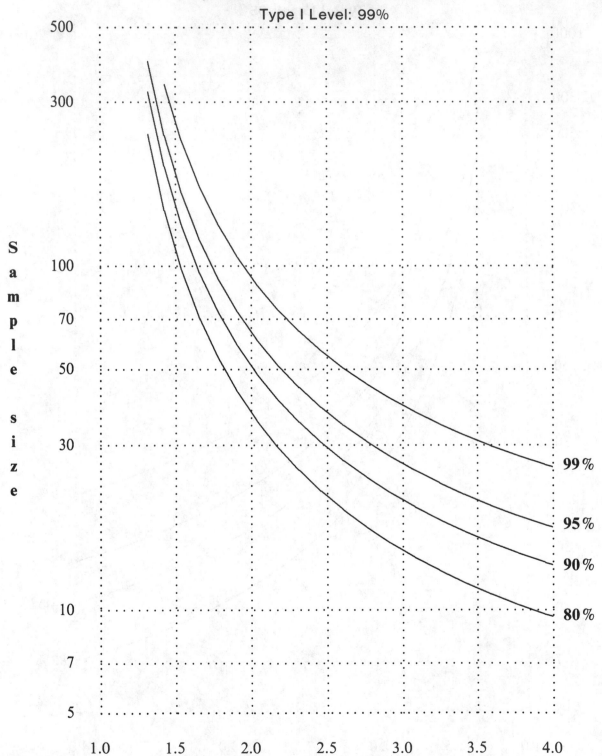

Ratio of hypothesized variances

Percentages on curves are Type II levels

Figure 62

MINIMUM SAMPLE SIZES
Normal Tolerance Intervals
.90 Population Proportion

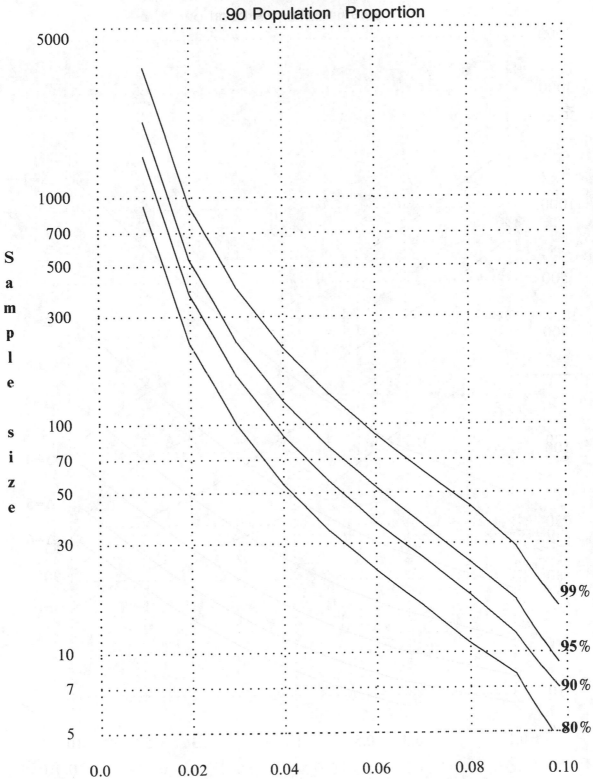

Population increment

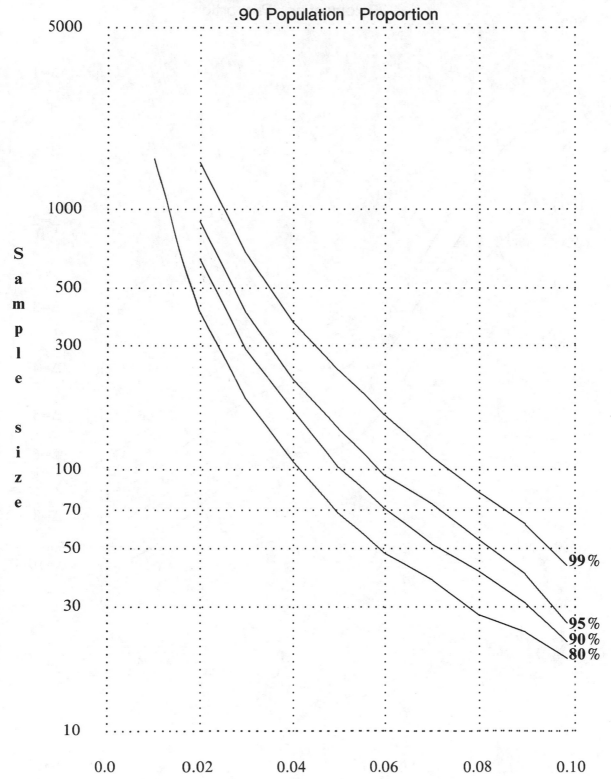

Figure 59

MINIMUM SAMPLE SIZES
Nonparametric Tolerance Intervals
.90 Population Proportion

Population increment

Figure 60

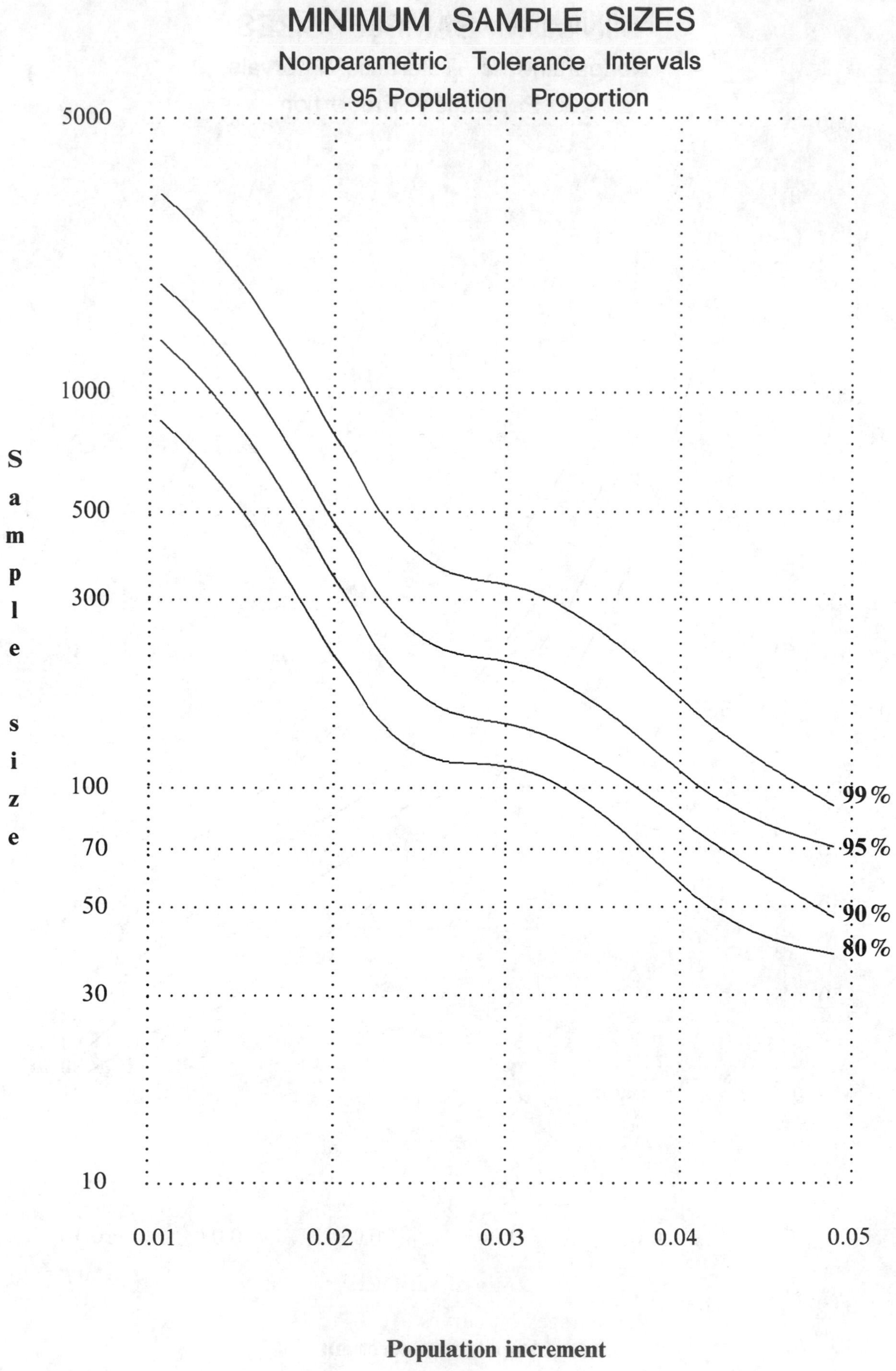

MINIMUM SAMPLE SIZES
Nonparametric Tolerance Intervals
.95 Population Proportion
5000
1000
500
300
100
70
50
30
10
Sample size
99%
95%
90%
80%
0.01
0.02
0.03
0.04
0.05
Population increment

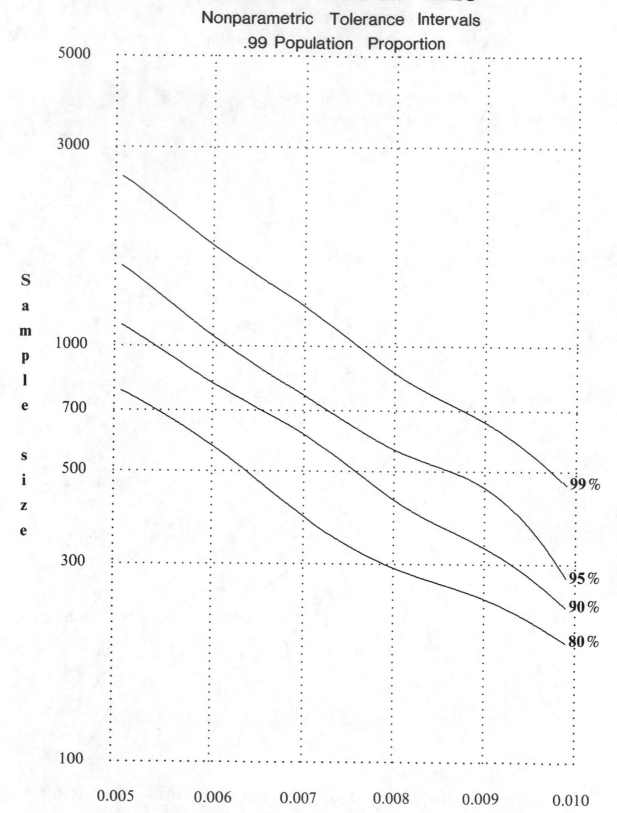

Figure 61

MINIMUM SAMPLE SIZES
Nonparametric Tolerance Intervals
.99 Population Proportion

Population increment

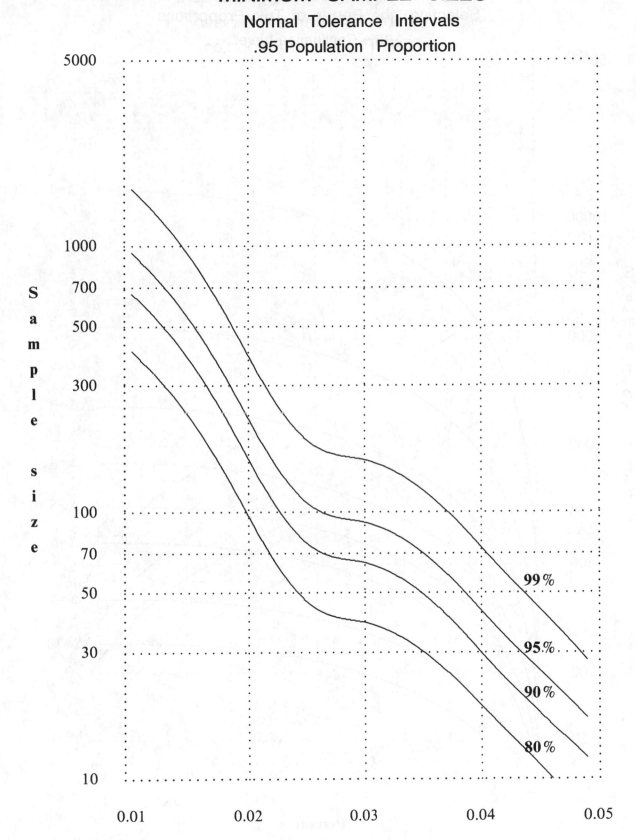

Figure 63

MINIMUM SAMPLE SIZES
Normal Tolerance Intervals
.95 Population Proportion

Population increment

107

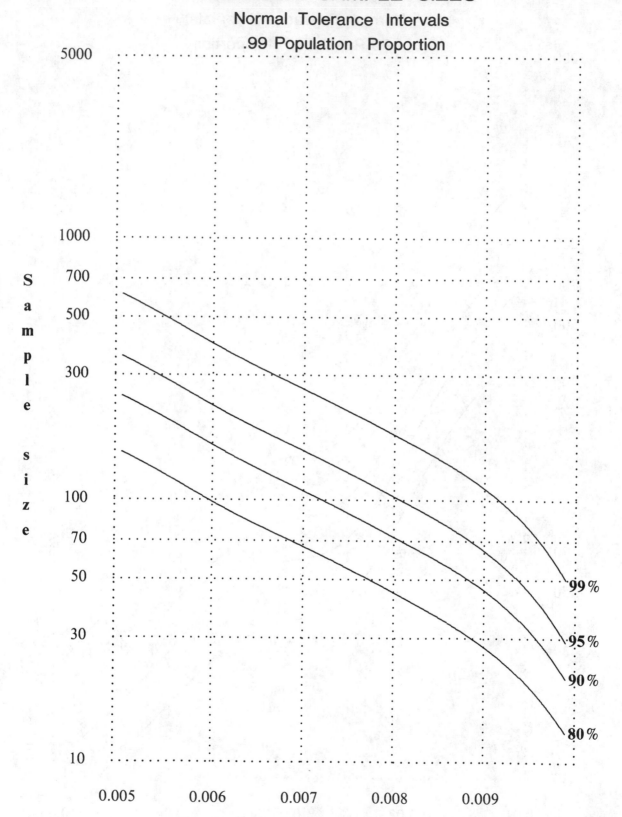

Figure 64

MINIMUM SAMPLE SIZES
Normal Tolerance Intervals
.99 Population Proportion

Population increment

Figure 65

Economic Optimization

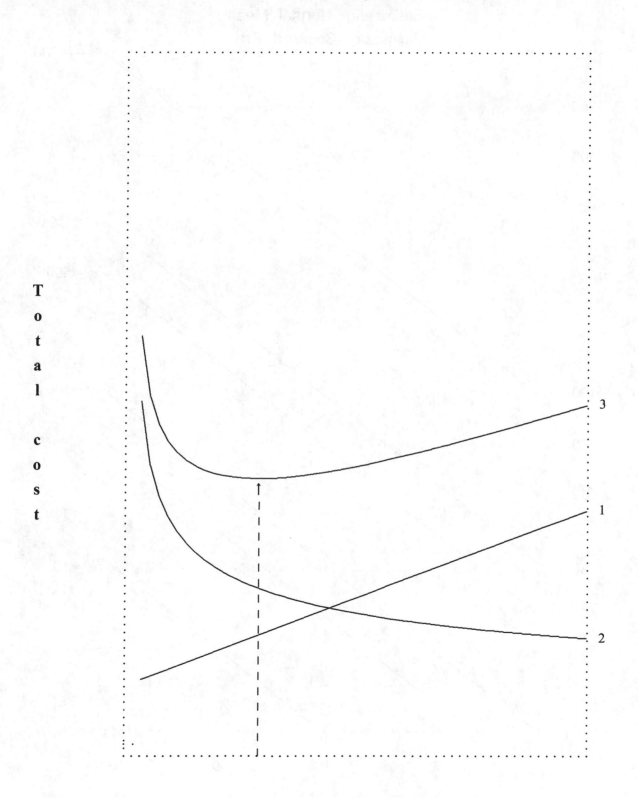

Total cost

Sample size

109

Figure 66

MINIMUM SAMPLE SIZES
Estimating Normal Mean
Minimizing Squared Error

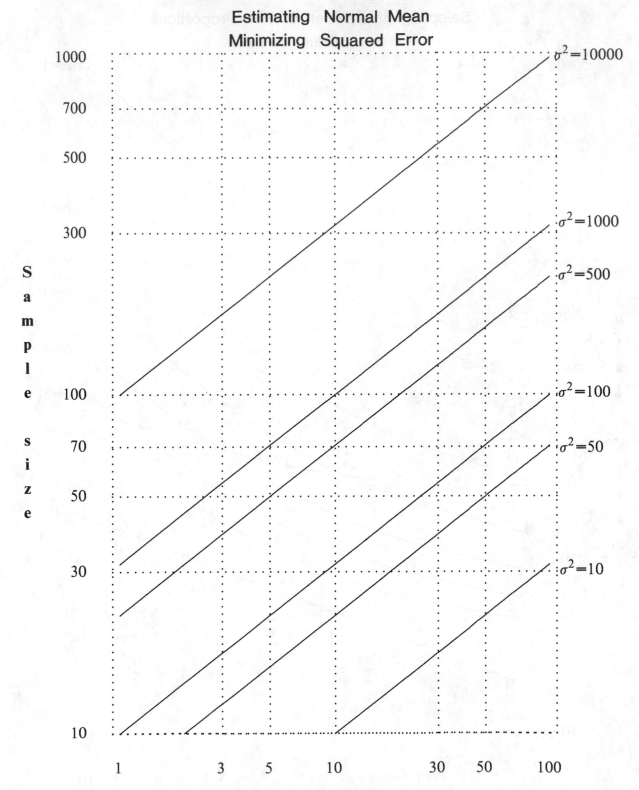

Figure 67

MINIMUM SAMPLE SIZES
Estimating Normal Mean
Absolute Deviation

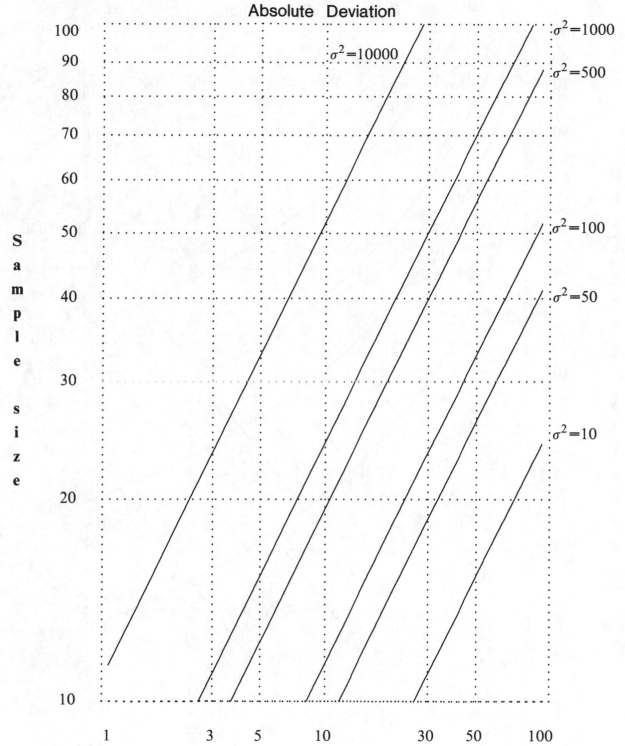

Cost ratio

Figure 68

MINIMUM SAMPLE SIZES
Selecting Better Normal Mean
Economic Optimization

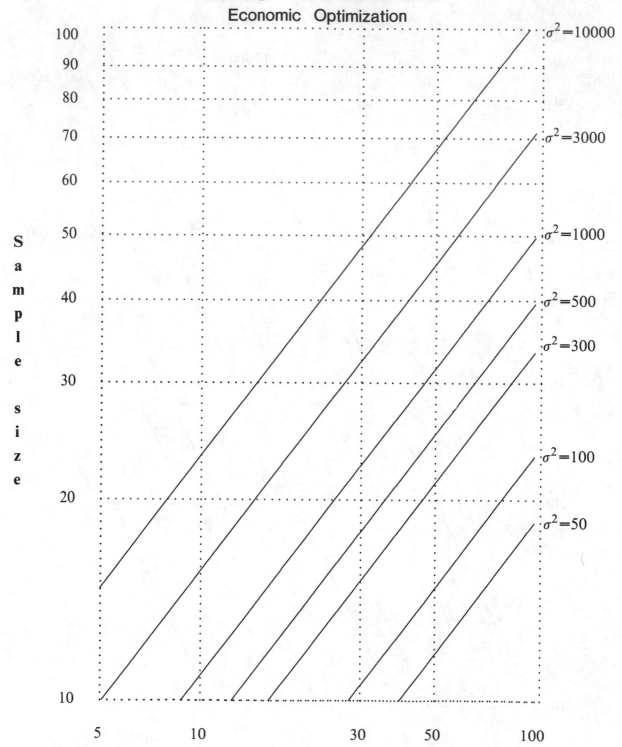

Cost ratio

Figure 69

MINIMUM SAMPLE SIZES
Selecting Better Proportion
Economic Optimization

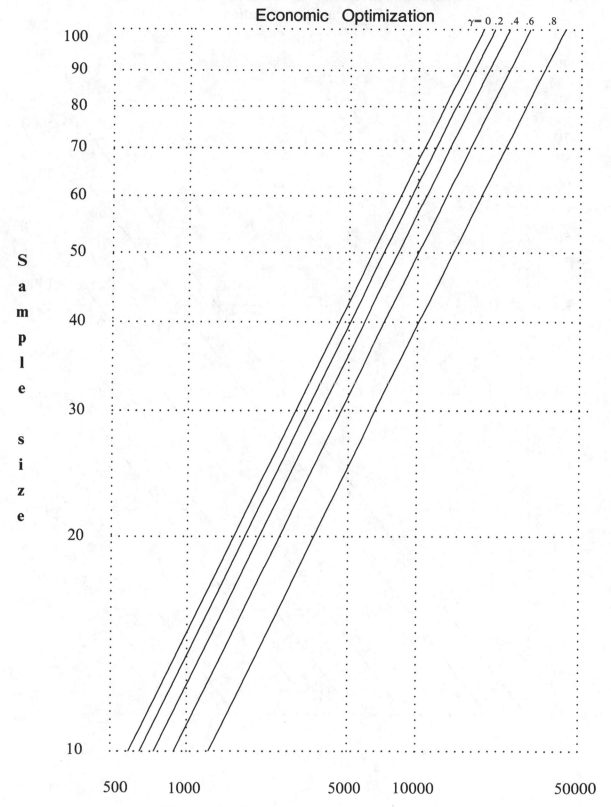

Cost ratio

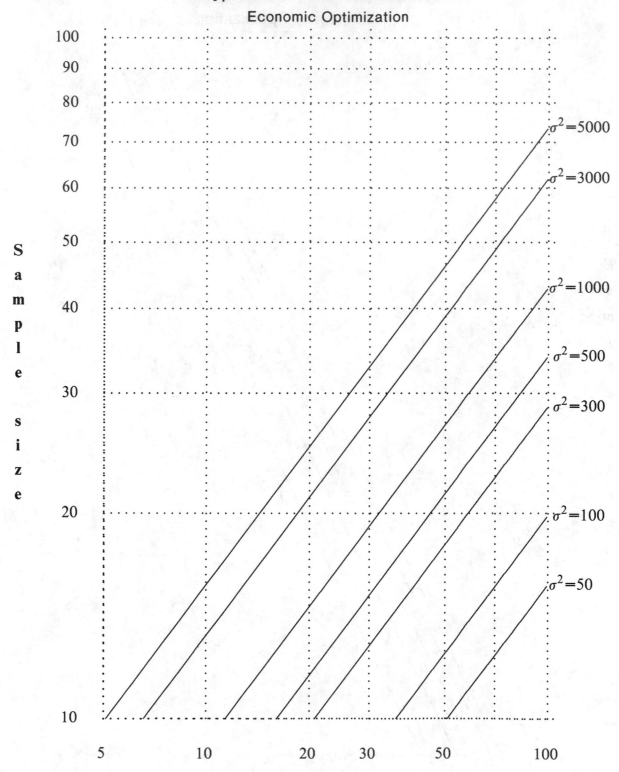